# What others are saying about
## *Twelve Keys to Developing Spiritual Maturity*

RICHARD MOORE has captured the doable essence of developing spiritual maturity. His foundation of scriptures and words of apostles and prophets, illustrated by engaging stories, brings the reader into an edifying reading experience that can motivate true change in the reader's life.

—Jack R. Christianson, author and director of the Orem Institute of Religion

THIS WORK IS A DELIGHTFUL COMBINATION of doctrinal epiphanies and humorous yarns, masterfully woven together in a way that only Rich Moore can! Dr. Moore provides much-needed context for the doctrine of being born again, while helping his readers to both assess their state of spirituality and place their hope in Christ's merciful gift of Atonement. Twelve Keys to Developing Spiritual Maturity is a must-read!

—Alonzo L. Gaskill, assistant professor of Church History and Doctrine, Brigham Young University

# 12 KEYS

## TO DEVELOPING

## SPIRITUAL
## MATURITY

*FOR CAREY,*
*I hope you enjoy the book*

*Richard G Moore*

# 12 KEYS

## TO DEVELOPING

## SPIRITUAL MATURITY

Achieving our Divine Potential

Richard G. Moore

CFI
Springville, Utah

ISBN 13: 978-1-55517-942-8
ISBN 10: 1-55517-942-8

Published by CFI, an imprint of Cedar Fort, Inc., 925 N. Main, Springville, UT, 84663
Distributed by Cedar Fort, Inc. www.cedarfort.com

LIBRARY OF CONGRESS CATALOGING-IN-PUBLICATION DATA

Moore, Richard G., 1952-
  Spiritual maturity / by Richard G. Moore.
    p. cm.
  Includes bibliographical references and index.
  ISBN-10: 1-55517-942-8 (alk. paper)
  ISBN-13: 978-1-55517-942-8 (alk. paper)
  1. Christian life--Mormon authors. 2. Spiritual formation. I. Title.

  BX8656.M663 2006
  248.4'89332--dc22

2006021833

Cover design by Nicole Williams
Cover design © 2006 by Lyle Mortimer
Printed in the United States of America

10   9   8   7   6   5   4   3   2   1

Printed on acid-free paper

# Dedication

For Mom and Dad

# Table of Contents

# Acknowledgments

I would like to thank my friends and co-workers John Thompson, Ted Gibbons, Steve Linford, and Mike Roberts for reading over rough drafts of my manuscript and suggesting valuable and needed changes and additions. Thanks to Cedar Fort for taking a chance on a no-name author. And special thanks to my wife, Lani, for encouraging and believing in me.

# Introduction

WHERE'S A SUPERHERO WHEN you really need one? Sprawled across the bed in my basement bedroom, my cousins and I contemplated this question. I was raised in a small town in Utah—a wonderful place to grow up. Everyone in town knew everyone else in town. I played peanut-league baseball, built rafts to sail on the pond, rode horses with friends, and was blissfully battered playing no-pads, no-helmet tackle football on the park lawn.

I spent many hours of my early youth (probably too many) poring over the exploits of comic book superheroes. My favorites were Batman and Spiderman, but I also enjoyed the adventures of Flash, Superman, and others.

In the world of superheroes, some inequalities were apparent to me even at an early age. For example, the vast majority of superheroes lived and worked somewhere on the East Coast. Few were in the western part of the United States, none that I knew of lived in Utah, and there was definitely no superhero in my hometown. My concern had to do with the safety of my community.

We didn't have a single superhero, and our entire police force consisted of a guy named Cliff. Cliff was a farmer during the day, but he emerged in the evenings as our community's law enforcement. Cliff the cop patrolled each night from six to ten (eleven-thirty on weekends). Given his schedule, my young mind grasped the frightening possibilities. The probability of major crimes in our community loomed large, especially during the day or after ten at night (eleven-thirty on weekends).

I lived just off Main Street, in the heart of the action, and my two younger cousins lived only a block away. After discussing my concerns with my cousins, we decided we needed to do something. If our town had no superheroes, we would become superheroes.

For a while we tried to copy the superheroes with whom we were familiar, but a towel tied around your neck and a cutout "S" pinned to your chest doesn't make you Superman. And wearing red pajamas and running down the street as fast as you can does not make you the Flash, although it does prompt some interesting looks from neighbors.

Disappointed by our efforts, we met to rethink the situation. In our basement headquarters, we hatched a scheme that excited us with its possibilities. We would create our own completely new superheroes. And so it was that I became Treeman, aided by my younger assistants, Branch and Twig. The big, old tree in my backyard became our headquarters. We designed our own costumes, including capes, masks, and utility belts. We practiced for hours swinging from ropes tied to the limbs of our tree headquarters, and we converted an old barn into a superhero gymnasium. We set up bogus bad guys and threw sticks, Treeman's favorite weapon, at the targets.

I am proud to say that if people checked the records of our little community during my era as Treeman, they would find no major incidents of criminal activity, no crime waves. In fact, they would discover that there was little crime at all. No thanks are necessary. We were just happy to help.

Why the trip down memory lane? Because I don't do the Treeman thing anymore. And the reason is not that they cut down my tree or because both of my cousins grew to be a lot bigger than I, which meant that I would have had to be a Twig. The reason is I grew up.

As we get older, some aspects of maturity seem to develop almost automatically. Physical maturity just happens. The experiences of life tend to mature us intellectually, regardless of our formal schooling or training.

Social maturity may not come as naturally as physical development, but the more interaction we have with people, the more our social skills grow and develop. Life's experiences have a way of sobering us and helping us see things through more mature eyes. While it is true that some people mature more than others, maturing seems to be a natural process of life.

However, there is one area where the maturing process does not happen naturally. In fact, the natural man is an enemy to this process. Spiritual maturity does not come automatically with age, or even with life's experiences. Spiritual maturity must be worked at, developed, and earned as a reward for spiritual effort. Working with youth and young single adults for years has shown me that in some cases, children are more spiritually mature than their parents, often because the young people pay a price that their parents had never paid.

The Apostle Paul said, "When I was a child, I spake as a child, I understood as a child, I thought as a child: but when I became a man, I put away childish things" (1 Corinthians 13:11). It is time for many of us to grow up spiritually, not to put away *childlike* things but to put away *childish* things. Spiritual maturity does not come quickly or all at once—it is a process.

That process is what this book is about. It contains principles and doctrines found in the scriptures and in the writings of latter-day apostles and prophets. I have also included some of my life's experiences, good and bad, that have been part of my spiritual schooling. I have used personal examples because they are what I know best and because life is a series of lessons from which we learn and grow. Unfortunately, many people do not learn from life's lessons, or they fail to see the truths being taught by the Great Teacher. We need to become observers of life—our own and the lives of others. When we do this, we begin to see lessons and parables and gospel truths all around us.

Of course, our schooling continues throughout this life and beyond. The Prophet Joseph Smith said that we wouldn't comprehend all this during this life and that "it will be a great while after you have passed through the veil before you will have learned them [the principles of the gospel]."[1]

The prophet Mormon was a master at looking at experiences of life and history and recognizing lessons to be learned. As he abridged the large plates of Nephi into what is a hefty part our present-day Book of Mormon, he often pointed out truths he wanted us to understand. After relating an incident, he would write, "thus we see" or "now we see," and then give us instruction as to what we should learn from the story. Only by using life as it is meant to be—a learning experience—will we begin to grow up in the gospel and develop spiritual maturity.

Gospel truths and principles, if learned and followed, will help us develop spiritual maturity. Because this process takes time and is revealed to us line upon line and precept upon precept, the principles discussed in this book are by no means comprehensive or complete. These are simply some of the keys I have discovered that assist our spiritual development. Clearly, I do not speak for The Church of Jesus Christ of Latter-day Saints. Any truths contained in this book come from the Lord through living prophets and the whisperings of the Spirit. Any errors are mine.

Notes

1. Smith, *Teachings of the Prophet Joseph Smith*, 348.

# 1

# Spiritual Maturation
# Is a Process

I HAD AN INTERESTING experience early in my career teaching for the Church Educational System. We were studying the Book of Mormon that year, and I was preparing for a lesson about the importance of spiritual rebirth. As I read through the scriptures listed in the lesson outline, I became confused about what it means to be born again.

There was no doubt in my mind that spiritual rebirth was an important step in the process of returning to the presence of God and receiving eternal life. The Savior made that clear when he spoke to Nicodemus:

> Jesus answered and said unto him, Verily, verily, I say unto thee, Except a man be born again, he cannot see the kingdom of God.
>
> Nicodemus saith unto him, How can a man be born when he is old? can he enter the second time into his mother's womb, and be born?
>
> Jesus answered, Verily, verily, I say unto thee, Except a man be born of water and of the Spirit, he cannot enter into the kingdom of God. (John 3:3–5)

If a person cannot even see the kingdom of God without being born again, then it is vital that this experience take place. What confused me was what the people said after King Benjamin asked them if they believed the words he had spoken. "And they all cried with one voice, saying: Yea, we believe all the words which thou hast spoken unto us; and also, we know of their surety and truth, because of the Spirit of the Lord Omnipotent, which has wrought a mighty change in us, or in our hearts, that *we have no more disposition to do evil, but to do good continually*" (Mosiah 5:2; emphasis added).

At the time I mistakenly understood this to mean that this group of people had overcome all temptation and did nothing but good from that moment. Considering the fact that I continued to struggle with temptation in my life and still succumbed to sin, albeit not major transgressions, a startling possibility occurred to me. Had I not been born again? I had been raised in a strong LDS home and baptized at age eight. I had received the Aaronic Priesthood, served in various leadership positions, graduated from seminary, received the Melchizedek Priesthood, been endowed in the temple, served a mission, and been sealed to my wife in the temple. At the time I was preparing for this lesson I was serving in a bishopric and teaching seminary. How could I go through all of that and not be spiritually reborn?

But there it was in the scriptures: a mighty change had been wrought in the hearts of the Nephites, and they had "no more disposition to do evil, but to do good continually."

I could not recall a mighty change taking place in my life. I don't remember being or feeling much different after I was baptized. And except for a stronger testimony and various growing experiences, I didn't see much of a difference between the premission and postmission me. With no mighty change and still struggling to be good continually, I suddenly feared that I had not been born again and, unless I could do something about it, I would not be allowed to enter the kingdom of God.

Honestly concerned about my salvation, I asked a teaching colleague, "Do we always know if we have been spiritually reborn." His reply was, "Oh, if you don't know, it hasn't happened."

That answer did not help my anxiety level. Nevertheless, I taught my lesson on spiritual rebirth as best I could, sticking to the doctrine, principles, and quotes found in the lesson manual and then moving on to the next lesson. But my personal search and study about the mighty change, the baptism of fire, spiritual rebirth, and true conversion continued over the next several months.

One day I was reading in 3 Nephi when I came across a scripture that helped me greatly in my understanding of being born again. After the great destruction that took place among the Book of Mormon people at the time Jesus Christ was crucified and near the end of the three days of darkness, the survivors heard the voice of the Savior speaking to them. Among other things He said, "And whoso cometh unto me with a broken heart and a contrite spirit, him will I baptize with fire and with the Holy Ghost, even as the Lamanites, because of their faith in me at the time of their conversion, were baptized with fire and with the Holy Ghost, *and they knew it not*" (3 Nephi 9:20; emphasis added).

Jesus spoke of Lamanites who had been baptized with fire and with the Holy Ghost but did not know it. After reading that verse, I realized that a person could be born again and be unaware of it. Maybe these Lamanites did not recognize the change in themselves because it was a gradual change. Perhaps a *mighty* change is not necessarily a *major* change or even a noticeable change but simply a very important change.

Another set of verses that affected my understanding of spiritual rebirth and helped me come to an understanding that it is a process rather than an event is found in Moses 6:

> That by reason of transgression cometh the fall, which fall bringeth death, and inasmuch as ye were born into the world by water, and blood, and the spirit, which I have made, and so became of dust a living soul, even so ye must be born again into the kingdom of heaven, of water, and of the Spirit, and be cleansed by blood, even the blood of mine Only Begotten; that ye might be sanctified from all sin, and enjoy the words of eternal life in this world, and eternal life in the world to come, even immortal glory;
>
> For by the water ye keep the commandment; by the Spirit ye are justified, and by the blood ye are sanctified. (Moses 6:59–60)

I was already familiar with likening physical birth to spiritual rebirth. When an infant is born into mortality, there is water, spirit, and blood. When someone is spiritually born again, water (baptism), spirit (the Holy Ghost), and blood (the atoning blood of Jesus Christ) again play crucial roles. But as I read the scripture this time, I stretched the analogy a little further. When a physical birth takes place, the result is a baby. When we are spiritually reborn, we become a spiritual infant.

I began to understand. I had been expecting myself to be a spiritual adult immediately following my spiritual rebirth. However, I began to realize that after we are born again, we must then be responsible to grow and mature through spiritual childhood and adolescence until, ultimately, we become a fully mature, spiritual adult—a god.

Why do I continue to struggle and fail in my attempts to keep all of God's commandments? Because I am a spiritual toddler, and toddlers fall down. It is not enough to be born again; we need to grow up spiritually. King Benjamin's people were not perfected on the day they experienced that mighty change of heart. The scriptures don't say that the people who had been listening to King Benjamin's sermon completely changed at that moment and never sinned again; rather, the scriptures state that they had no more disposition to do evil. Their hearts had changed. The Spirit had caused a change in their attitudes, desires, and intents. They had a sincere desire to do good continually.

Did they ever sin again? Yes, because they were still in a fallen mortal condition with all the weakness that brings.

Each of us has had moments in our life, after a powerful spiritual experience or a moving general conference session, when we said to ourselves, "I feel so motivated to be good. I'm going to be better from now on. I don't ever want to sin again." We may be completely sincere about these feelings, and our lives may improve dramatically, but we can't manage living the perfect lives we desire. This kind of spiritual maturity does not come in an instant. It is a process that began in our premortal life and continues throughout our mortal existence and beyond.

Elder Bruce R. McConkie wrote that "for most members of the Church the spiritual rebirth is a process that goes on gradually. The faithful are sanctified degree by degree as they add to their faith and good works."[1]

On another occasion Elder McConkie said that "if we begin the process of spiritual rebirth; . . . if we chart a course of sanctifying our souls, and degree by degree are going in that direction; . . . even though we have spiritual rebirth ahead of us, perfection ahead of us, the full degree of sanctification ahead of us, if we chart a course and follow it to the best of our ability in this life, then when we go out of this life we'll continue in exactly that same course."[2]

Speaking of the need to endure to the end, Elder Neal A. Maxwell taught that "the very process of being born again spiritually is not a one-time occurrence. Hence, Paul said that he died 'daily' (1 Corinthians 15:31). Such is the process of putting off the old self as one becomes a woman or a man of God."[3]

Whether we see being born again as something we begin in this life and then complete after this life, something that can happen to us again and again, or something that necessitates growing up spiritually afterward, it is a process. President Ezra Taft Benson spoke of this process as being "a step-by-step, steady and consistent movement toward godliness." President Benson also cautioned us that we must "not become discouraged and lose hope. Becoming Christlike is a lifetime pursuit and very often involves growth and change that is slow, almost imperceptible."[4]

The important thing for us to do during our mortal probation is begin the spiritual-rebirth process by getting on the right path. The Prophet Joseph Smith said that "being born again, comes by the Spirit of God through ordinances."[5] Then, after beginning that path through faith in Christ, repentance, and baptism, we must "press forward with a steadfastness in Christ, . . . feasting upon the words of Christ, and endure to the end" (2 Nephi 31:20). Elder McConkie reinforced this concept when he wrote, "Spiritual rebirth begins and ends with belief in Christ. When repentant souls turn to Christ and seek a new life with him, the processes of rebirth commence. When their belief in the Lord increases until they are able to do the works that he does, 'and greater works than these' (John 14:12), their rebirth is perfect, and they are prepared for salvation with him."[6]

Our spiritual maturity can be measured by how often and to what degree we enjoy the influence of the Holy Ghost. Our goal should be to have the Holy Ghost as a constant companion. In this step-by-step process of receiving a fulness of spirituality, we can follow specific steps to help us in our quest. The chapters that follow will look at these steps, or keys, to spiritual maturity, which include being obedient, exercising responsible stewardship, accepting the will of God, learning the doctrine, doing the right thing for the right reason, stability, balance, handling adversity well, seeking the Spirit, and enduring to the end.

Notes

1. McConkie, *The Promised Messiah*, 351.
2. McConkie, *Doctrines of the Restoration*, 54.
3. Neal A. Maxwell, "If Thou Endure Well," Brigham Young

University fifteen-stake fireside, December 2, 1984, 4.

4. Ezra Taft Benson, "A Mighty Change of Heart," *Ensign*, October 1989, 5.

5. Smith, *Teachings of the Prophet Joseph Smith*, 162.

6. McConkie, *Doctrinal New Testament Commentary*, 3:401.

# 2
# Obedience

I'M NOT SURE WHO the first person in our dispensation was to say, "Obedience is the first law of heaven." However, with Joseph F. Smith, George Q. Cannon, S. Dilworth Young, N. Eldon Tanner, Bruce R. McConkie, Ezra Taft Benson, Joseph B. Wirthlin, and other general authorities repeatedly making the statement through the years, we can be certain that obedience *is* the first law of heaven.

In Doctrine and Covenants, section 59, the Lord says, "Blessed are they whose feet stand upon the land of Zion, who have obeyed my gospel; for they shall receive for their reward the good things of the earth, and it shall bring forth its strength. And they shall also be crowned with blessings from above, yea, and with commandments not a few, and with revelations in their time—they that are faithful and diligent before me" (vv. 3–4).

Notice that the Lord tells us that He is going to crown us not only with blessings but also with "commandments not a few." Unfortunately, some of us do not see commandments as blessings. People speak with joy and gratitude about being showered with blessings from God, but I haven't heard many people express excitement about being showered with commandments.

Spiritual maturity can be determined, in part, by how we look at commandments. The immature might see God's commandments as hindrances to life's fun, while the spiritually mature individual sees commandments as a manifestation of our Heavenly Father's love for His children, as a way to help us return to His presence, and as guardrails lining the road to exaltation. When viewed properly, obedience to God's commandments is seen as enhancing our joy and happiness. "Behold, I say unto you, wickedness never was happiness" (Alma 41:10).

The spiritually mature also recognize that obedience provides greater freedom. This may be a little difficult for some people to see. I certainly did not understand this during most of my teenage years. The principle is this: the more obedient I am to God's commandments, the more I will be trusted by my Father in Heaven. And the more trusted I am, the greater freedom He will offer me as a reward.

I actually began to understand this principle during my senior year of high school. Prior to this, my relationship with my parents was not always smooth. We did not see eye to eye on many issues. One evening during the summer before my senior year, things kind of boiled over. I felt that I was a mature, responsible young man and should be given more independence. I was bothered that I had to tell my parents where I was going, what I was going to do, who I would be with, and what time I would return home. I could not see why I had a set time to be home each night and why I had to check in with my parents when I arrived home.

We went a few rounds on this topic. I gave Mom and Dad my best teenage arguments, including an emotional display. I got all the parental clichés in return. The one thing I had the most difficulty understanding was my father's logic that if I would be more obedient, I would have more freedom. At the time, I felt that the more I followed their rules and guidelines, the less freedom I would enjoy. In fact, I feared their strictness would eliminate all of my freedoms.

I remember one evening going to my room feeling quite angry. That night I devised a plan to prove how wrong my parents were. I would become the ideal child. If Dad said, "Be home by ten-thirty," I would roll in by 10:15. If Mom asked, "Will you please take out the garbage?" I would reply, "Already did!" I would do everything they asked of me—and more. Then, after graduation, I would confront them, saying, "I have been totally obedient this year. Do I have more freedom? Have I become more independent because I have demonstrated my responsibility? No! I have had *no* freedom! But now I declare my independence! Good-bye."

I smiled as I thought about it. The plan was a good one. I'd show them, and they would be sorry.

Although my motives were far from pure, my actions of obedience brought about a positive change in our home. We rarely had any disagreements, and my relationship with my parents improved significantly. Occasionally I would take a break from the pleasantness and remind myself why I was doing this. *Sure, things are going great and they are happy,* I would think. *Why shouldn't they be? I'm their little slave!* For the most part, however, I just enjoyed the year and the harmony within the home.

On a Wednesday evening in April, I was at the high school involved with an extracurricular activity when my friend stopped by to say that he couldn't give me a ride to school in the morning. "Sorry," he said, "but you'll have to ride the bus." Riding the bus may have been exciting when I was young, but for a senior, it was the ride of shame, announcing to the world, "I have no car."

Dreading the thought of having to take the bus, I asked, "Why can't you give me a ride?"

"My brother and his family are moving to a town just outside of Las Vegas, and I am going to drive a truck filled with their stuff to their new home." Then he added, "When I finish helping them move in, my brother said I could borrow his car and drive into Las Vegas."

"Wow. I've never been to Las Vegas."

"Me neither," he replied. "It's going to be great because not only will I be in Las Vegas, but I'll also be driving a '67 Camaro."

He got the envious look from me he wanted, and then an idea popped into his mind. "Come with me," he invited. "I'll only be gone for a few days."

"A few school days," I reminded him. "There's no way my parents will let me leave school and go to Las Vegas."

"It wouldn't hurt to ask. Let me know in the morning. It will be fun."

I wasn't even going to ask my parents, but as I drove home that night I decided to go ahead and try. This would be the final straw, the proof I was waiting for to show them that after all I had done, I still didn't have any freedom.

When I got home, everyone in the house had gone to bed. I turned off the clock light over the stove. My mom always left it on with instructions for the last person home to turn it off. That way, if she woke up in the night, she could look at the clock in the kitchen and know whether everyone was safely home. Of course, we still had to check in with Mom and Dad as well, but sometimes those conversations were so brief, and my parents were so sleepy, that in the morning they didn't remember even talking to me.

On this particular night, I stood at the door of their bedroom and went through the ritual. "I'm home," I whispered.

I heard a sleepy "okay," which was the typical reply from Mom.

But this night, I added, "Can I go to Las Vegas in the morning with Boyd?"

Silence followed for a moment, and then my mom said, "Okay."

And that was it. I had permission that I believed would stand up in a court of law. As I began to step quietly from the room, my dad's voice came out of the dark. "Rich?"

"Yeah," I replied, believing it was over.

"There's a twenty on my dresser—take it."

"Okay."

I picked up the twenty and made my way down the stairs to my bedroom in the basement. I sat on my bed cross-legged and stared at the twenty-dollar bill. *What's going on?* I pondered. And then I began to get angry. *They're not going to let me go to Las Vegas. This is a cruel joke.* I had received permission from sleeping parents, but in the morning that permission would be withdrawn by parents who were fully awake.

I pictured the scene in the morning:

"How come you're not ready for school?" my mom would ask.

"I'm not going to school."

"Why? Are you sick?"

"No, I'm going to Las Vegas with Boyd. We talked about this last night, and you said I could go."

"Las Vegas? You've never said anything about going to Las Vegas. And I never would have given you permission to go. Now get ready for school or you'll be late."

"But Mom, you said . . ."

About that time I imagined my dad would come out of the bedroom saying, "Where's my twenty, you little thief?"

Yup, it was going to be ugly, but I would follow through because it was as good a time as any to throw my lack of freedom in their faces. Irritated, I got into bed and finally fell asleep.

In the morning, I wasn't as angry, but I was apprehensive about the forthcoming confrontation. I came up the stairs and walked quietly into the kitchen. My mom was cooking breakfast.

"What time are you leaving today?" she asked.

"For where?" I said, a little defensively.

"I thought you were going to Las Vegas with Boyd."

She didn't seem upset. Maybe she was going to let Dad lower the boom, the old good parent/bad parent routine. "I've got to call him to find out for sure, but I think we'll be leaving at about ten," I answered.

"How long are you going to be gone?"

"Just a couple of days."

"A couple of days?" my dad said, coming out of the bedroom. *Here we go,* I thought. But he opened his wallet and handed me another twenty. "You might need some more money," he said. I was stunned. I felt like demanding, "All right, who are you and what have you done with my real parents?"

My dad must have noticed my surprise. "You do know why we're letting you go, don't you?" I didn't answer. He continued, "You've shown us this past year that you are responsible and that you can be trusted. Here's some of that freedom you wanted. We're letting you go because we trust you and we know you won't do anything foolish or anything that you or we would be ashamed of."

I went to Las Vegas with Boyd. We had fun, and we didn't do anything that would bring shame to us, our parents, or our Father in Heaven. I never confronted my parents with my lack of freedom. In fact, as I thought back over that year, I realized there had been many things they had let me do and a lot of things with which I had been trusted. I began to wish I had learned this lesson earlier in my youth.

Elder Boyd K. Packer said it this way:

> Obedience to God can be the very highest expression of independence. Just think of giving to him the one thing, the one gift, that he would never take. . . . Think of giving him that one thing that he would never wrest from you. Obedience—that which God will never take by force—he will accept when freely given. And he will then return to you freedom that you can hardly dream of—the freedom to feel and to know, the freedom to do, and the freedom to be, at least a thousandfold more than we offer him. Strangely enough, the key to freedom is obedience.[1]

Obedience to gospel principles is like being inside an hourglass and moving up. At first it can appear as if many freedoms are being restricted. *You must do this. You cannot do that.*

Many people believe that conforming to God's laws limits their freedom. They feel uncomfortable because they are unwilling to change. Quite a number of us actually choose commandments to ignore because we do not want our lives restricted in certain areas. But if we will continue in obedience and faith, we will emerge into a world of newfound freedoms.

An obedient person is free to attend the temple and receive saving ordinances, free to serve a mission, free to have a marriage and family sealed for eternity, free to call upon or use the power of the priesthood, free to feel the Spirit, free to receive personal revelation from the Lord. These are a few of the freedoms only the obedient ever know. Faithful people move into a realm that the unrighteous never experience. The key to all these freedoms is obedience. Obedience is the first law of heaven and opens the door to greater spiritual maturity and awesome spiritual freedoms.

Notes

1. Packer, *That All May Be Edified*, 256.

# 3

# Responsible Stewardship, Spiritual Stability, and Selfless Service

WHEN THE SALT LAKE Valley-bound pioneers of the Martin and Willey handcart companies were trapped in Wyoming in the fall of 1856 by an early snowfall, Brigham Young acted immediately. He told the congregation gathered at the Bowery on Sunday, October 5:

> Tomorrow our semi-annual conference commences. . . .
> I will now give this people the subject and the text for the
> Elders who may speak today and during the Conference,
> it is this . . . many of our brethren and sisters are on the
> plains with handcarts, and probably many more are now
> seven hundred miles away from this place, and they must
> be brought here, we must send assistance to them. The
> text will be—to get them here! . . . This is my religion; that
> is the direction of the Holy Ghost that I possess, it is to
> save the people. . . . I shall call the Bishops this day, I shall
> not wait until tomorrow, nor until next day, for sixty good
> mule teams and twelve or fifteen wagons. . . . I will tell you
> all that your faith, religion, and profession of religion, will

13

never save one soul of you in the celestial kingdom of our
God, unless you carry out just such principles as I am now
teaching you.[1]

The Saints of the Salt Lake Valley rallied and organized a relief effort
that saved many lives.

We can learn many lessons from this episode in Church history. I
wish to focus on two. First, Brigham Young and others with an appointed
stewardship over the Church responded swiftly and with deep care and
concern. They recognized their assigned stewardship and acted responsi-
bly. Second, the Saints who organized and traveled on the rescue mission
performed acts of sacrifice and service based on the understood stewardship that we are all brothers and sisters, and we are all responsible to help
those in need.

Membership in The Church of Jesus Christ of Latter-day Saints provides many opportunities for service. Most members of the Church who
are actively involved in their wards and stakes have callings. These callings
come from the Lord and are stewardships over which we are given responsibility.

Because we are all at varying levels of spiritual maturity, we will see the
entire gamut from slackers to super servers working in most wards. Some
people will not accept callings, while others faithfully serve in several positions at the same time. Some people accept callings but then do very little,
if anything, in their stewardship. Others magnify their callings to the best
of their abilities.

When I served as a bishop, I referred to those who were responsible in their callings as the pillars of the ward. Wards are built on a few
strong, faithful families and individuals who take their stewardships seriously. While we might wish we could clone a few of these pillars, it's much
better to have individuals develop, grow, and step up their service to pillar
status.

I remember when I decided to be a faithful, hard-working member
of the Church. Part of that decision came as a result of watching my parents; another part of my resolve came while I served as a missionary and
watched members in small branches. Some were dependable, while others
never took any responsibility. I told myself that when I returned home, I
would always be someone that ward leaders could count on.

That resolve was put to the test within months after I arrived home
from the mission field. I received a letter in the mail from a member of the

stake high council inviting me to clean ditches on the stake welfare farm; the letter had been sent to fifty elders. The assignment was one month away, and I decided that I would be there on that designated Saturday morning.

One month later, I was out with friends very late on a Friday night. When I got home, I found a note on my bed from my mother, reminding me of the ditch-cleaning project, which was now only a few hours away. *Oh, no,* I thought. *I don't want to clean ditches in the morning, especially after only a few hours' sleep.* I thought it over and, pushing away the guilt as best I could, decided that with all of those other elders helping out, I would not be missed.

I made sure that my alarm was turned off and hopped into bed. My alarm clock may have been silenced, but at 5:30 that morning, my guilt alarm went off. I tried to ignore my feelings of obligation. I was so tired. However, after a few minutes, I surrendered to my sense of responsibility and got up, got dressed, and drove to the stake farm, where I was greeted by the entire crew: the high councilor who sent the letter and a friend of mine who had been home from his mission almost a year. That was it.

Two out of fifty responded to the assignment. My higher math skills tell me that is a 4 percent turnout. I would have been missed! The three of us cleaned ditches for much of the day, and I was glad I had gone. I felt a bond with this sincere high councilor and the faithful, responsible elder who had served with no wavering, no shirking of responsibility. I still see him once in a while, and he has not changed. Currently, he serves as a stake president.

The Church needs more people like him—more men and women who are pillars in the kingdom of God. An individual who accepts and magnifies callings with a positive attitude and, without being compelled, anxiously engages in good causes and does things to help others, is showing signs of spiritual maturity.

The more spiritually mature a person becomes, the more stable, steadfast, firm, and trustworthy he will be. Far too many members of the Church are tossed to and fro and come in and out of activity as if the Church were a revolving door. Church members need to develop stability. Those Latter-day Saints who are always there, who serve whenever and wherever they are called, demonstrate spiritual maturity. These pillars in wards and stakes magnify their callings and add strength to the quorums and auxiliaries throughout the Church.

Other characteristics of stability in the kingdom of God include dependability, consistent efforts to be obedient, and an attitude of continuous repentance. Prayerful evaluation of these qualities in our own lives will help us measure our personal spiritual stability.

Elder Richard R. Lyman, an early twentieth century apostle, once commented on one of the outstanding characteristics common to all who had served as presidents of The Church of Jesus Christ of Latter-day Saints—their dependability. "These men so lived and so conducted themselves that they had nothing to conceal. Their lives were like the contents of an open book. Such men say what they mean and mean what they say. Their outstanding characteristic is dependability."[2]

I was raised by a father who was dependable. If he said he was going to do something, he would do it. I remember him going to the welfare farm to dig potatoes when he was not feeling well. I was going with him and suggested he not go. "We're going," he said. "I told them I would be there." And off we went.

I did not always appreciate my father's dependability when I was young because he expected me to be as reliable as he was. The summer after I graduated from high school, I got a job working at the Brigham Young University dairy farm. During hay season, the eighteen-wheelers loaded with bales of hay arrived at the farm from daylight on. I spent several days unloading and stacking hay in the barns. Wire-tied bales weighed between one hundred and one hundred twenty-five pounds; outside temperatures were in the 90s and even warmer in the barns.

One evening we finished unloading the last truck when the boss announced that there might be another truckload of hay coming. He told me to go home but stay by the phone in case they needed me. I promptly drove home and took the phone off the hook! Pleased with myself, I sat on the floor with a cold lemonade and watched television. My dad came home from work, saw the phone, and asked me why it was off the hook. I explained to him the situation and told him how exhausted I was and why I wanted to make sure that no one could call. I expected him to understand!

Dad told me to call the dairy farm immediately. When I couldn't get through, he told me to drive out to the dairy and see if the hay truck had arrived. I tried to argue, but he made it clear to me that when I had taken the job I had accepted all the responsibilities that came with that job, not just punching the clock and putting in my time. He expressed concern over the lack of dependability I was demonstrating to my employers, and he was sad that I had not learned to be responsible.

I drove back to the dairy farm and discovered that another hay truck had arrived. My boss was happy to see me and told me later that I was one of the most dependable young men who had ever worked for him. Although I was not the responsible person he believed me to be, I set a goal to become as reliable as my father.

The greater a person's spiritual maturity, the greater the degree of his obedience and covenant keeping. "I will go and do the things which the Lord hath commanded," said a young but spiritually mature Nephi (1 Nephi 3:7).

And consider the premortal example of Jesus when He volunteered to follow His Father's plan and offer himself as a sacrifice. He said, "Here am I, send me" (Abraham 3:27). Even without being assigned or commanded, the spiritually mature will "do many things of their own free will, and bring to pass much righteousness" (D&C 58:27).

Because of our fallen condition, we all sin; we all "come short of the glory of God" (Romans 3:23). But our efforts to be obedient need to be consistent. We need to be loyal to the Lord Jesus Christ, whose name we have taken upon ourselves through baptism. God knows our hearts, and if our honest intent is to do that which is good, we are on the right path, even if it takes time for all of our actions to match our righteous intentions.

Repentance is more than forsaking transgressions and seeking forgiveness. Repentance is the mighty change of heart from a sinful, fallen nature to a disposition in which our desire is to always do the right thing. A person who home teaches every month, never missing a family, can still repent in the area of home teaching. He may need to better prepare worthwhile messages for each family. Perhaps he needs a deeper feeling of appreciation and love for the families he visits. Doing whatever he needs to do to be a better home teacher is repentance. In this instance, repentance does not mean overcoming transgression; it means improvement, growth, and spiritual development.

We sometimes hear people say they went through a growing experience. The process of spiritual growth is the process of repentance. This is why we must continually repent. Continual repentance means we are pressing forward on the pathway to perfection.

We can gain a sense of our spiritual maturity by evaluating our spiritual stability. Do we recognize that we are capable of being a slacker in the kingdom if we become casual in our prayers, scripture study, service, and obedience? Are we dependable in all things? Is our obedience consistent? Finally, are we constantly repenting, not only of our sins but also of our imperfections?

My father is retired and lives in a little cul-de-sac where the city snow-plow does not go. When it snows, Dad gets up early and drives his little tractor around the neighborhood, clearing driveways and sidewalks before his neighbors leave for work. He has not been assigned by the Church to do this, and these neighbors are not the people he home teaches. He does not charge anyone a fee for this service, and he doesn't want anything in return. He simply enjoys serving others.

Part of being responsible in the kingdom of God is understanding that we do not have to be officially assigned to reach out a helping hand. As children of our Father in Heaven, we are all brothers and sisters, with an inherent stewardship to do all we can for each other.

After Cain had murdered his brother Abel, the Lord spoke to Cain and asked, "Where is Abel, thy brother? And he said: I know not. Am I my brother's keeper?" (Moses 5:34). The answer to Cain's question is, "You are responsible for the welfare of your brother." Or, better said by BYU professor Chauncy Riddle, "No, Cain, you are not expected to be your brother's keeper. But you are expected to be your brother's brother."[3]

The most important way we can serve God is to righteously serve His children, our brothers and sisters. One Father's Day when I was a little boy, I wanted to give my father something special, something that showed my love for him. I can't remember what I ended up choosing, but I do remember the prayer I uttered the night before that memorable Father's Day.

I began, "Dear Heavenly Father," and then I stopped because it occurred to me that I had a Heavenly Father and I had not given Him anything for Father's Day. I remember apologizing in my prayers and wishing him a happy Father's Day. When I climbed into bed that night, I thought about what I could have given my Father in Heaven. My young mind was puzzled. After all, what do you give the man who has everything? And even if I came up with a good idea for a present, how can you give anything to God?

As years went by, I came to believe that my thoughts that night were simply the product of the mind of a naïve little kid. I told myself not to worry about it because you cannot give God anything. But I was always a little troubled when Father's Day or Christmas rolled around because it seemed that the individuals who mattered most were being ignored. The answer to my dilemma came shortly after I got married.

When my wife and I married, we lived in a basement apartment. I was going to school full time and working part time, and we had little money to cover our expenses. In fact, my wife even dropped out of school for a short time to help support us as I finished school.

My parents lived about half an hour away, and on occasion, we would drop by to visit and eat. During one of those visits, Dad took me aside and said, "I wonder if you might be able to do me a favor. I went shopping the other day and accidentally bought an extra case of soup. Our food storage area is pretty filled up, and we have no place to put this case of soup. We can't use it, and I don't know what to do with it. Could you take it?"

"Sure," I replied. "I'm happy to help."

We took the soup, and I was pleased twofold. We got food we could use, and I was able to help out my dad. A few weeks later on another visit to my parents, I discovered that my dad had made another shopping error, and we went home with a number of items that wouldn't fit in the freezer. This went on until I began to worry about Dad. Perhaps Mom should do all the shopping; Dad didn't seem to be able to handle it very well.

Around Easter we traveled to my parents' home for a family get-together. When we were getting ready to return to our apartment, my dad took me aside and said, "I came home from the supermarket the other day with an extra ham. We've already got the one, so we don't need it. Could you and Lani use a ham?"

Well, I'm no dummy. You can only fool me for six or eight months. Extra case-lot items are one thing, but who would accidentally buy too many hams? "Sure, we'd love to take the ham," I said, and then with a look that would let him know that I knew what he was up to, I added, "Now, how much do I owe you?"

"You don't understand. I'm giving it to you."

"I understand completely," I said, taking out my wallet. "Let me pay you back."

He paused for a couple of seconds, looked at me, and said, "You can't possibly pay me back."

"Sure I can. I just got paid."

"I don't care how much you got paid. You could still never pay me back."

I was thinking that must be some expensive ham when my dad clarified, "It's not just the ham or the soup or the other things we've given you. It's all the things over the years that your mom and I have done for you. It's the sacrifice and time and energy and money and worries that we have invested in you. You will never be able to pay us back for all we've done for you."

My father is not the kind of guy who fishes for compliments or appreciation, and I was pretty sure he wasn't asking me to pay him back on some kind of monthly installment plan. Because he doesn't normally talk this way, I knew he was serious and was trying to make a point. But if there was no way I could ever pay Mom and him back, what could I do?

It was like he read my mind. "Do you know why we do these things for you? One reason is that we love you and your sisters, and we want to help when we can. The other reason is to pay back *our* parents for everything *they* did for us. But there is something you can do to pay us back," he continued. "Someday you do something for your own kids when they need help. That's the way it works."

My dad was right—that is the way it works. Since having my own children, I have realized that when schoolteachers or people at Church do something nice for my kids, I feel as if they have done something nice for me.

There is no area where this concept rings truer than in our relationship with our Heavenly Father. We can never pay Him back for all He has done and continues to do for us. What does an all-knowing, all-powerful being need from us? King Benjamin tells us:

> If you should render all the thanks and praise which your whole soul has power to possess, to that God who has created you, and has kept and preserved you, and has caused that ye should rejoice, and has granted that ye should live in peace one with another—
>
> I say unto you that if ye should serve him who has created you from the beginning, and is preserving you from day to day, by lending you breath, that ye may live and move and do according to your own will, and even supporting you from one moment to another—I say, if ye should serve him with all your whole souls *yet ye would be unprofitable servants.* (Mosiah 2:20–21; emphasis added)

If we can never pay Him back, what can we do? We can serve Him by serving His children. Jesus said, "Inasmuch as ye have done it unto one of the least of these my brethren, ye have done it unto me" (Matthew 25:40). We serve God by doing things for others: family, friends, neighbors, and strangers. All are spirit children of God. "And behold, I tell you these things that ye may learn wisdom; that ye may learn that when ye are in the service of your fellow beings ye are only in the service of your God" (Mosiah 2:17).

God's work and glory is "to bring to pass the immortality and eternal life of man" (Moses 1:39). When we take upon ourselves the name of Christ, we also take upon ourselves that same work. The spiritually mature will bear one another's burdens, mourn with those who mourn, and comfort those who stand in need of comfort (see Mosiah 18:8–9). They will fulfill their duties diligently, magnify their callings consistently, and serve others selflessly. Maturing spiritually is part of the process of becoming steadfast and immovable—pillars in the kingdom of God. "Him that overcometh will I make a pillar in the temple of my God, and he shall go no more out" (Revelation 3:12).

Notes

1. Young, in *Journal of Discourses*, 4:113.
2. Richard G. Lyman, in Conference Report, April 1934, 109.
3. In Holland, *On Earth As It Is in Heaven*, 142.

# 4

# Accepting the Will of God

I USED TO REFER to what Nephi, son of Helaman, received from the Lord as ultimate prayer power. I thought that Nephi had reached a level of spirituality so high that God would simply give him anything that he asked. My thinking was based on Helaman 10:5, which reads, "I will make thee mighty in word and in deed, in faith and in works; yea, even that all things shall be done unto thee according to thy word." My misinterpretation of this scripture came as a result of my misunderstanding of the principle of prayer.

I was raised in the Church by wonderful parents who taught me how to pray. However, at some point I began to regard prayer as the method used to get Heavenly Father to help me receive the things I wanted. The concept was simple in my mind: if I prayed and received what I wanted, I had prayed with faith. Conversely, if I did not receive the blessing I sought, I had not prayed with enough faith.

A closer look at a few verses in Helaman 10 provides a better understanding of Nephi's level of obedience to the Father's will. Yes, Nephi was an extremely righteous man, but he did more than merely pray with faith.

In verse 4 the Lord says, "Blessed art thou, Nephi, for those things which thou hast done; for I have beheld how thou hast with unwearyingness declared the word, which I have given unto thee, unto this people. And thou hast not feared them, and hast not sought thine own life, *but hast sought my will,* and to keep my commandments" (Helaman 10:4; emphasis added).

Nephi's desire to do the will of God was so great that he was not intimidated by what other people thought or by his own mortal inclinations. When the Lord said, "thou hast not sought thine own life," he was saying to Nephi, "Even at times when I have asked you to do something that you may not have wanted to do, you did not seek to do your own will. You always did what I wanted you to do."

It is not that God would now grant Nephi everything that Nephi wanted. It is that Nephi had so aligned his will with the will of the Lord that he would never ask for anything that God could not grant. "For thou shalt not ask that which is contrary to my will" (Helaman 10:5).

So one purpose of prayer is to gain blessings from God—the blessings He wishes us to have. Therefore, another purpose of prayer is to help us discover God's will for our lives so that we can align our wills with His. As we do this, we reach a level of spiritual maturity where we want what He wants for us.

This is what the Savior did. "I have suffered the will of the Father *in all things* from the beginning" (3 Nephi 11:11, emphasis added).

A student in one of my institute classes helped me make this discovery. During a discussion about prayer, he shared with the class a few lines about prayer from the Bible Dictionary:

> Prayer is the act by which the will of the Father and the will of the child are brought into correspondence with each other. The object of prayer is not to change the will of God, but to secure for ourselves and for others blessings that God is already willing to grant, but that are made conditional on our asking for them. Blessings require some work or effort on our part before we can obtain them. Prayer is a form of work, and is an appointed means for obtaining the highest of all blessings.... We pray in Christ's name when our mind is the mind of Christ, and our wishes the wishes of Christ—when his words abide in us. We then ask for things it is possible for God to grant.

> Many prayers remain unanswered because they are not in
> Christ's name at all; they in no way represent his mind, but
> spring out of the selfishness of man's heart.[1]

This student may never know how much of an influence the things he said had on me. These words were an answer to a long-standing prayer of my soul, an answer that opened my understanding and healed my wounded heart.

In her youth, my mother played softball and tennis and went swimming nearly every day during the summer. She was healthy and strong. However, I never knew that person. Early in her married life, Mom became very ill, and I have no memory of my mother ever being well. Among many health problems, she suffered from asthma, which made breathing extremely difficult. I remember her coughing and coughing; sometimes she would even kneel on the floor and lean over the bed while she coughed. On several occasions, she coughed so hard that she actually broke her ribs. She saw doctors, took medications, and faced almost constant physical distress, which she rarely shared with anyone. She went on with her life as though nothing was wrong. Despite her illnesses, she was happy and caring and funny—a joy to be around.

During the time I served as a missionary, Mom nearly died. Thankfully, she pulled through and regained a semblance of health. As years passed, more serious health problems appeared. I had become used to the fact that she was not well, but I was disturbed by the alarming rate of this rapid decline in what little health she had enjoyed.

My job brought my family back to the area where my parents lived; our new home was only about five miles away from where I grew up. I spent a considerable amount of time with my parents, often stopping by for a few minutes on my way home from work. Our children visited Grandma and Grandpa often, and because my mom was small, they called her "Teeny Grandma."

As the holiday season approached one year, my mom took a dramatic turn for the worse. She had already spent time in the hospital, but she did not appear to be recovering. One morning before I went to work, my dad telephoned and asked if I would come by and help him give my mom a blessing. He had already administered to her several times during the past few months and felt that another blessing would help. Leaving our children with a neighbor, my wife and I drove to my parents' home.

My dad invited me to seal the anointing and pronounce the blessing. I accepted, and we helped Mom to a chair in the bedroom. Dad anointed her head with consecrated oil. Then we placed our hands upon her head, and I began to seal the anointing and give her a priesthood blessing. Prior to this, I had learned by experience not to have any preconceived notions about what to say. I wanted to be prepared to say whatever the Spirit dictated.

On this particular morning, I did not know with certainty whether my mother was going to be healed, but my personal desire for her to be made well had a powerful influence upon my mind. As I began the blessing, impressions came. I felt that Father in Heaven loved Mom, that He was mindful of her, and that He would be with her. The impression that followed was so strong that an actual phrase came into my mind: *In a short time, the pain you are experiencing will be nothing but a memory.*

I repeated the phrase aloud as part of the blessing. At that moment, I thought, *My mom is going to be made well. Perhaps in a few weeks, she will be completely healed, and all this will simply be a memory of a difficult time.* I said a few more things, but my mind could not get over the phrase that I perceived to be a promise that she would completely recover. I finished the administration filled with hope.

A week or so later, my mother returned to the hospital. Still, I believed it was only a matter of time before she would be home and well. The doctors were not as hopeful, but they were not aware of the blessing. My mom's brother, who was also her stake president, visited her hospital room and also gave her a blessing. In that blessing, she was told that she would be home for Christmas, which was less than two weeks away.

Our family decorated her hospital room with a tree and ornaments and other Christmas decorations. Doctors wanted to keep her a few more days to watch for problems. They said she could go home in time for Christmas if there were no complications. The following day, her condition worsened, and she was transferred to the intensive care unit. With heavy hearts, my father and I took down the decorations from her hospital room. We realized that she would not be home for Christmas.

Over the next few days, the situation grew bleaker. On Christmas Eve, a doctor told us he didn't think she would survive the night. Late on Christmas Eve, I sat alone with my mom in her hospital room. I did not understand what was happening. What about the blessing that I had given her? What about the stake president's blessing? The thought struck me, could the blessing have meant not that she would be back in her own home for Christmas but that she would be "taken home to that God who gave [her] life?" (Alma 40:11).

I was horrified. I knew that all people must die. However, it had never seriously occurred to me that my mother would not recover from this illness. I slid from my chair onto my knees by the side of her bed and prayed that Heavenly Father would spare her at this time. I begged that my mother would not be taken from me at Christmas time. I wondered how I could ever enjoy the Christmas season again if each year it conjured up images of my mother's death, the mortuary viewing, the funeral, and the painful loss. I knew that others had lost loved ones at Christmas time, even on Christmas day for that matter. They had accepted this as a difficult part of life and moved on. However, I did not believe I was strong enough to cope with this. "Not now," I pleaded. "Please, not now."

My mom did not pass away on Christmas. In fact, she rallied to the point that she was removed from the ICU. There was even talk of her being released from the hospital. Nevertheless, our hopes were dashed again as her condition worsened and she was returned to the intensive care unit.

This was a difficult time for me. Not only was I facing the possibility of losing my mother, but I was also experiencing a personal crisis of faith. Many questions repeatedly crossed my mind. Had there not been many people praying and fasting for my mother? Had she not received a number of priesthood blessings? Was not my mom one of the most faithful and obedient people I had ever known? Why was our Father in Heaven not hearing our prayers? Or worse, was God hearing our prayers and not responding? I had been taught and still believed that Heavenly Father hears and answers all prayers, but I now wondered why He was not answering mine.

I felt that my life was becoming a sham. Each day I would go to work and teach my seminary classes that daily prayer was important, that we could take our problems to our Father in Heaven because He loves us and will help us. But I didn't feel that I was loved. At night when my wife asked if we were going to pray together before going to sleep, I sometimes replied, "Go ahead and pray if you want, but I don't feel like it. Maybe He will listen to you, but God doesn't listen to me."

With my own faith faltering, I became angry at the rest of my family. They listened to the hopeless picture painted by the doctors and believed it. They seemed resigned that Mom's death was certain. I told myself that she had gone through difficult illnesses before and recovered, and she could get well again. She was only fifty-nine years old! I complained to my wife that the entire family, immediate and extended, had given up. "Where is everybody's faith?" I asked bitterly, even as my own faith, belief, and hope dwindled.

Early in February, my mother slipped into unconsciousness for several days. Family members spent nights at the hospital at her bedside. Doctors told us day after day that she could not possibly last through the night, only to have her prove them wrong night after night. However, the end of her mortal life seemed inevitable. I was still so confused about why this was happening after all the prayers and fasting and priesthood blessings. I began wondering if my own lack of faith was the reason she was not recovering.

Early one afternoon, I was in the ICU waiting room when my father entered. He announced that Mom had regained consciousness and had requested that I give her a blessing to release her from this life.

"I can't do that, Dad."

"That's what she wants, Rich," my dad said quietly. "She asked me to give her a blessing, and now she wants you to give her one."

I followed my father to my mom's room in the ICU. We closed the door, and I approached her hospital bed. She held my hand.

"Is this what you really want?" I asked.

"I want you to give me a blessing and release me from this life," she said, "because it is the right thing. It is time for me to go."

I put my hands upon her head, and my dad placed his hands on mine. I gave her a priesthood blessing and released her from this mortal life. It was the most difficult blessing I have ever given. When I finished she thanked me and hugged me. Even in her weakened condition, I could feel the squeeze of her arms.

I asked her if she was afraid. She shook her head and said, "Not at all."

For the first time in weeks, I felt at peace; I felt the Spirit. I was not angry with my family, and I was not bitter at God any more. The Spirit told me that it was my mother's time, and I felt that I could let her go. I knew I would miss her, but I also knew that everything would be okay. I was so thankful for these feelings.

Two days later I stood in the hospital room and watched my mother slip away. At that moment of the greatest sorrow I had ever felt, I also experienced a tremendous sense of peace. I was struck by the thought that for the first time in more than thirty years, my mom was not suffering from pain or illness. I still did not understand why my prayers had not been answered the way I wanted, but I felt that it was meant to be and so I was comforted.

The day my institute student shared the insights about prayer from the Bible Dictionary affected me powerfully. When class ended, I went to my office and read the words again and again. I had known that we are not to pray for things that are wrong, but it had never occurred to me that asking for my mother to be made well could be wrong. How could praying for the life of a righteous person to be spared be a wrong thing? It was not a bad thing I was asking. But could a seemingly good thing be a wrong thing if it is against God's will?

I had not sought God's will in the matter because I was so caught up in what I wanted. Pieces of the puzzle started to come together. The priesthood blessing I had given her promised that in a short time her pain would only be a memory. As she crossed from mortality into the spirit world, that blessing was fulfilled. Elder Russell M. Nelson taught:

> Each one of us has the power to heal cuts, bruises, broken bones, and virtually everything that comes our way. At the same time, a process of self-destruction has been built into each body. We know this as the aging process. It gives absolute insurance and assurance that the marvelous self-healing powers of the body can never prevail over the plan of our Creator. Healing cannot destroy the great plan of happiness, which allows our privilege of returning to the presence of God.[2]

It also dawned on me that my mother did not need a priesthood blessing to release her from this life. Thousands of people leave this mortal sphere without any kind of official release. "Why did my mom request a blessing?" I asked. The answer? She did not need the blessing, but I did. Unlike the rest of my family, I had been unable to accept God's will.

Mom had not asked for a blessing so she would be able to pass away, but so I might come to understand and accept God's will. The blessing had been for me. It was humbling to recognize that my mother's last mortal act was to teach me to accept the will of God.

Because of this feeling of humility, I was finally beginning to understand what she had been trying to teach me. Humility is the key to moving past our own willful nature and submitting ourselves to the will of the Lord. Our spiritual maturity can be measured by our willingness to freely submit to God. Humility is recognizing the difference between our own will and the will of our Father in Heaven, and then acknowledging God's will is right and accepting His will as our own. The Prophet Joseph Smith proclaimed, "Whatever God requires is right, no matter what it is, although we may not see the reason thereof till long after the events transpire."[3]

Praying "Thy will be done" and truly meaning it may be the most difficult—and most important—prayer we will ever offer. This prayer demonstrates tremendous faith and puts us well on the path toward true spiritual maturity.

Notes

1. Bible Dictionary, s.v. "Prayer," 752–53.
2. Russell M. Nelson, "Twenty Questions," address to religious educators, September 13, 1985, 5.
3. Smith, *Teachings of the Prophet Joseph Smith*, 256.

# 5
# Learning the Doctrine

AND JESUS INCREASED IN wisdom and stature, and in favour with God and man" (Luke 2:52). During the Savior's mortal life, He matured physically, socially, spiritually, and intellectually. Notice that the scripture does not state that He increased in *knowledge* but rather in wisdom. Knowledge certainly is an important part of wisdom, but to simply know things is not enough. Wisdom is the proper use and application of truth. We can possess knowledge of many things, even many truths, but still lack wisdom. Lucifer is a prime example of this principle.

Commenting on the difference between knowledge and intelligence, Elder Dallin H. Oaks wrote:

> In inspired words now embodied in the scriptures of the Latter-day Saints, the Prophet Joseph Smith taught that "whatever principle of intelligence we attain unto in this life, it will rise with us in the resurrection." (D&C 130:18.) What is meant by intelligence is not mere knowledge, by whatever means it is acquired. This is evident from the following sentence: "And if a person gains more

knowledge and intelligence in this life through his diligence and obedience than another, he will have so much the advantage in the world to come." (D&C 130:19.)

Note that intelligence is something more than knowledge. And note also the implication that knowledge is obtained by diligence, and intelligence is obtained by obedience. Admittedly, the two methods are not mutually exclusive. But we come close to an important mystery of the gospel when we understand that the intelligence God desires us to obtain is much more than knowledge, and it cannot be obtained without obedience and revelation. That is the Lord's way, and it is far beyond the ways of the world.[1]

What, then, is the intelligence God desires us to obtain? More specifically, what are we to learn while we are here upon the earth? The Lord said:

And I give unto you a commandment that you shall teach one another the doctrine of the kingdom.

Teach ye diligently and my grace shall attend you, that you may be instructed more perfectly in theory, in principle, in doctrine, in the law of the gospel, in all things that pertain unto the kingdom of God, that are expedient for you to understand;

Of things both in heaven and in the earth, and under the earth; things which have been, things which are, things which must shortly come to pass; things which are at home, things which are abroad; the wars and the perplexities of the nations, and the judgments which are on the land; and a knowledge also of countries and of kingdoms. (D&C 88:77–79)

This seems to invite us to learn as much as we can in as many areas as we can, as long as the information we are seeking is not trivial. However, we need to be aware that there is a hierarchy of importance of the things we choose to study. Elder Bruce R. McConkie wrote, "All types of knowledge, however, are not of equal worth, all do not reward the acquirer with equal progress toward exaltation."[2]

Elder Boyd K. Packer taught that the education of the intellect is not necessarily the crowning achievement of life. "It is time you learn, if you have not already, that there is a part of our nature, the part we term spiritual, that needs training as well. It is the spiritual part of our education that is most easily neglected. And consequently we see many who are academic and intellectual giants but morally are puny and stunted and diseased."[3] On another occasion, Elder Packer said, "True doctrine, understood, changes attitudes and behavior. The study of the doctrines of the gospel will improve behavior quicker than a study of behavior will improve behavior. . . . That is why we stress so forcefully the study of the doctrines of the gospel."[4]

The study of gospel doctrines and principles is the most important learning we can do, and the bulk of that study needs to be done individually and in our families. The Church provides meetings, such as general conference, sacrament meeting, Sunday School, Primary, Young Men and Young Women, priesthood, and Relief Society, where the gospel is taught. At firesides and seminary and institute classes, speakers and teachers can instruct us in the doctrines of the kingdom. But none of these meetings can replace the gospel teaching that should take place in our homes or the sweet instruction a person can receive in those quiet, peaceful moments of personal scripture study and prayer.

Elder Neal A. Maxwell wrote, "The need for greater individual study of the gospel—more scholarship on the part of individual members who do not demand of the Church that it supply them with intellectual handouts—is also something which can start to be met in the home. We can be much more effective as leaders and followers if we engage in individual gospel scholarship."[5]

Some people complain that they hear the same things again and again in our Church meetings. Others say, "There is no meat; there is no depth to the doctrines being taught!" I disagree; just think of the general conference addresses you've heard! However, I personally believe that the Church's responsibility is to teach basic gospel principles, while each individual Church member carries the responsibility to receive the deeper things of the kingdom through personal study, pondering, prayer, and revelation. The meat of the gospel appears to be reserved for those who become mature enough to receive it. "But strong meat belongeth to them that are of full age, even those who by reason of use have their senses exercised to discern both good and evil" (Hebrews 5:14).

The study of doctrines and principles should begin in the home with parents teaching their children the gospel in regular family home evenings, family scripture study, gospel discussions, and family prayer. Each parent needs to have personal gospel and scripture study so children see their parents as models for developing gospel scholarship.

I remember coming home at night and finding my mother sitting in the living room reading scriptures, studying Church history, or going over the latest general conference addresses. "Did you have a good time?" she would ask. "What did you do?"

After we talked for a moment about my evening, she would say, "Listen to what I have been learning tonight." I would sit down with my mom, and she would teach me the doctrines of the kingdom. Sometimes my already-late night would become even later as we discussed gospel principles for more than an hour before I finally went to bed. I loved those times.

Primary, Sunday School, seminary, and other meetings and programs sponsored by the Church were helpful. But as I look back on my life and the doctrinal knowledge I acquired before my mission, the vast majority came from my dad's family home evening lessons and my mom sharing what she was studying. Church programs assist parents in teaching the gospel; they are not meant to replace the family as the major source of gospel learning.

When the three-hour meeting block on Sundays was established, President Spencer W. Kimball said, "Recently we established the new consolidated schedule which is aimed at enriching family life even further, together with greater opportunity for individual and family gospel scholarship and for more Christian service."[6]

President David O. McKay also noted, "The testimony of the gospel is an anchor to the soul in the midst of confusion and strife. Knowledge of God and his laws means stability, means contentment, means peace, and with that a heart full of love reaching out to our fellow men, offering the same blessings, the same privileges."[7]

Stability in the Church is an aspect of spiritual maturity that is crucial to our salvation. It is especially important during the last days, an era of extreme wickedness.

From the Pearl of Great Price we read, "For in those days there shall also arise false Christs, and false prophets, and shall show great signs and wonders, insomuch, that, if possible, they shall deceive the very elect, who are the elect according to the covenant" (Joseph Smith–Matthew 1:22). How can the elect, those saved for the latter days who have made covenants with God in the waters of baptism and in the holy temples, avoid being deceived? The answer is found in verse 37. "And whoso treasureth up my word shall not be deceived" (Joseph Smith–Matthew 1:37).

How do we treasure up the word of God? First, we must know the word of God. We need to regularly study the standard works of the Church. We need to listen and follow the words of the prophets and apostles. We need to recognize the whispering of the Spirit and then follow the promptings we receive. Knowledge of true doctrines will protect us from being deceived by false doctrines. To mature spiritually, we must have an understanding of basic gospel principles "that we henceforth be no more children, tossed to and fro, and carried about with every wind of doctrine, by the sleight of men, and cunning craftiness, whereby they lie in wait to deceive" (Ephesians 4:14).

I have been in more than a few gospel doctrine classes when someone asked "Don't we believe . . ." The reply, "Don't you know what you believe?" comes to mind. Of course, we aren't expected to know all of the revealed doctrines of the Church, but many of us put little effort into becoming gospel scholars. Speaking to those called to serve in leadership positions in the Church, President Ezra Taft Benson said,

> You will not be able to intelligently discuss such matters with members unless you have set an example of personal gospel scholarship and study. You should know our Church history. Further, you should ensure that the scriptures are used to teach correct doctrines in priesthood, auxiliary, and sacrament meetings. In a word, we call upon you to encourage members to read and study the scriptures in an effort to strengthen their testimonies of this great latter-day work.[8]

A Church Educational System presentation states that the scriptures are simple enough for children yet challenging enough for prophets. In this life, we will never reach the stage where we understand all the depths and meanings of the standard works.

Elder Maxwell was a brilliant scholar and scriptorian. A few years before he passed away, he remarked, "I am excited to report to you that I am enjoying the scriptures more than ever. I have read a lot in my life—thousands of books, I'm sure. But rarely do I encore reading except for the holy scriptures."[9]

We should not be content with leaving gospel scholarship to the Brethren, BYU religion professors, or the few people in our ward whom we rely on to make sure that the doctrine being taught in our meetings is correct. Each of us has a responsibility to study and learn gospel principles and doctrines. Elder Maxwell wrote, "For a disciple of Jesus Christ, academic scholarship is a form of worship. It is actually another dimension of consecration. Hence one who seeks to be a disciple-scholar will take both scholarship and discipleship seriously; and, likewise, gospel covenants. . . . How else could one worship God with all of one's heart, might, *mind*, and strength?"[10]

A big part of knowing the doctrine comes from living what we know. Elder Oaks said, "Whereas the world teaches us to *know* something, the gospel teaches us to *become* something, and it is far more significant to *become* than it is to *know*."[11] Jesus taught that "if any man will do his will, he shall know of the doctrine" (John 7:17).

When we live a true principle, the Spirit bears witness to us that it is true. The Prophet Joseph Smith asserted that the Book of Mormon was the most correct book on earth, but simply knowing that does not move us closer to our Father in Heaven. A person who *abides by its precepts* draws nearer to God.[12]

As a missionary, I came across individuals who would say things like, "When I know the Word of Wisdom is really from God, then I'll live it," or "If I find out there really is a God, then I'll pray." My companion and I would try to explain that by living the commandments or by doing the will of God, we receive that confirmation.

At one point, I was teaching a woman who simply refused to pray. When pressed for her reasons for not praying, she finally admitted that she did not know if God existed and she felt foolish praying if it turned out no god was listening to her. We told her that there was no reason to feel foolish because we were the only people who would know that she had been praying and, more important, that God was there. We testified to her that our Father in Heaven exists and that she would feel much worse not praying and then later finding out that God was there all along. She was hesitant but agreed to at least consider praying.

A week or so went by, and then she came to the church one evening. As soon as she saw us in the hallway, she cried out, "Oh, elders, there is a God! There is a God!" Not being the most sensitive person in the world, I simply agreed with her: "Yeah, I know."

"But I didn't," she replied. "However, I prayed, and God answered my prayers. He really is there." What a sweet moment—followed by another sweet experience at her baptism a few weeks later.

Spiritual maturity increases when we learn gospel truths and then apply those truths to our lives. Having greater spiritual maturity will help us understand that our Father in Heaven has chosen not to reveal many eternal truths to us during our mortal existence. We may feel a sense of frustration at times because there are so many things that we do not know. As a gospel teacher, I respond almost daily to a student's question with, "I don't know" or "We are not really sure of the answer to that question because it has not been revealed to us by the prophet."

We also need to have the spiritual maturity to recognize that it is not wise to share all that we do know. Personal revelation is meant to be just that—personal. Often, we are tempted to share something that has been revealed to us through the Spirit, even though it was meant only for us. The prophet Alma taught, "It is given unto many to know the mysteries of God; nevertheless they are laid under a strict command that they shall not impart only according to the portion of his word which he doth grant unto the children of men, according to the heed and diligence which they give unto him" (Alma 12:9).

President Brigham Young was clear in this regard:

> There is one principle that I wish the people would understand and lay to heart. Just as fast as you will prove before your God that you are worthy to receive the mysteries, if you please to call them so, of the Kingdom of heaven—that you are full of confidence in God—that you will never betray a thing that God tells you—that you will never reveal to your neighbor that which ought not to be revealed, as quick as you prepare to be entrusted with the things of God, there is an eternity of them to bestow upon you. Instead of pleading with the Lord to bestow more upon you, plead with yourselves to have confidence in yourselves, to have integrity in yourselves, and know when to speak and what to speak, what to reveal, and how to carry yourselves and walk before the Lord.[13]

Part of spiritual maturity results from learning gospel principles and doctrines through diligent study, consistent prayer, and quiet pondering. It comes when we are not prideful because of our acquired knowledge but rather acknowledge that there is still much we do not know. And maturity grows when wisdom is exercised regarding which spiritual things are shared and which remain unspoken.

President Gordon B. Hinckley quoted the following passage from the Doctrine and Covenants: "That which is of God is light; and he that receiveth light, and continueth in God, receiveth more light; and that light groweth brighter and brighter until the perfect day" (D&C 50:24). He then said, "What a remarkable statement that is. It is one of my favorite verses of scripture. It speaks of growth, of development, of the march that leads toward Godhood."[14]

This growth toward godhood is the advantage referred to in another verse from the Doctrine and Covenants, which reads, "If a person gains more knowledge and intelligence in this life through his diligence and obedience than another, he will have so much the advantage in the world to come" (D&C 130:19).

## Notes

1. Oaks, *The Lord's Way*, 43.
2. McConkie, *Mormon Doctrine*, 426.
3. Packer, *Let Not Your Heart Be Troubled*, 28.
4. Boyd K. Packer, "Little Children," *Ensign*, November 1986, 17.
5. Maxwell, *A More Excellent Way*, 126.
6. Kimball, *The Teachings of Spencer W. Kimball*, 493.
7. David O. McKay, "What about Jesus Christ?" *Improvement Era*, December 1960, 905.
8. Benson, *The Teachings of Ezra Taft Benson*, 375.
9. Maxwell, "Sharing Insights from My Life," *Brigham Young University 1998–99 Speeches* (Provo, Utah: University Publications, 1999), 110.
10. Maxwell, "The Disciple-Scholar"; emphasis in original.
11. Ibid.; emphasis in original.
12. Smith, *History of the Church*, 4:461.
13. Brigham Young, in *Journal of Discourses*, 4:371–72.
14. Hinckley, *Teachings of Gordon B. Hinckley*, 303.

# 6

# Doing the Right Thing for the Right Reason

ONE MORNING DURING PERSONAL scripture study while serving as a missionary in Japan, I came across several verses from Doctrine and Covenants, section 50, that confused me. In verse 13, the Lord asks, "Unto what were ye ordained?" He answers the question in verse 14: "To preach my gospel by the Spirit, even the Comforter which was sent forth to teach the truth."

I thought I understood the importance of teaching by the Spirit, which to me meant that if I were keeping the commandments, living the mission rules, and teaching the outlined missionary discussions, I was teaching by the Spirit.

However, I became puzzled a few verses later when I read, "Verily I say unto you, he that is ordained of me and sent forth to preach the word of truth by the Comforter, in the Spirit of truth, doth he preach it by the Spirit of truth or some other way? And if it be by some other way it is not of God" (D&C 50:17–18).

How could a person teach "some other way"? It had never occurred to me that a missionary might simply be going through the motions of teaching people the gospel and not teaching correctly. I knew missionaries who didn't teach the outlined discussions. One of my earliest companions had designed his own lessons, but what he taught was still true, still based on scriptures and doctrine. Could that be "some other way"?

I had always assumed that teaching truth was teaching correctly, or teaching by the Spirit. Our Father in Heaven wants us to teach true doctrine, I reasoned, so as long as I am not teaching false doctrine, it has to be of God, doesn't it? But a rereading of verse 17 made it clear that the "word of truth" could be taught in some other way than by the Spirit. "And if it be by some other way it is not of God."

*How* the truth is taught may be as important as *what* is being taught. Is it possible that our reason for obedience to God's commandments is nearly as important as the obedience itself? As long as we are serving God, does it really matter why? Could our motivation for serving others be as important as the service?

While growing up, I admit, my motivation for obedience had often been the fear of being caught doing something wrong or the fear of punishment. But I had been obedient and figured that was the important thing. I had performed service in the neighborhood and in the Church based on a sense of responsibility or my dad making me go. I may not have always had the best attitude or much of a desire to serve, but I had served. Wasn't that enough?

After I had graduated from high school, I wanted to get away from home and be on my own. I was accepted to a university that was several hours away, and I was excited to move into an apartment with a few friends and become independent. It was invigorating to think I could get up in the middle of the night and go get a hamburger if I wanted. I never did, but because I had the freedom to do so if I wanted, I felt amazingly grown up. Although my lifestyle did not actually change much, the knowledge that I could do what I wanted was empowering.

One part of my life, however, did change—at least for a little while. When I lived at home with my family, I never missed any Church meetings. For the first few Sundays after I had moved away, I would wake up and say, "Nobody is here to make me go to Church! I don't have to go!" Then I'd get up, get dressed, and go to Church.

After a month or so, I began to exercise my new freedom in a negative way. I'd skip the earliest meetings and go later in the day to sacrament meeting. Even though I attended at least one meeting each Sunday, there was a definite decline in my spirituality. For the first time in my life, I was not totally active. As a result of my limited attendance, I did not receive any callings, I did not feel a part of my new ward, and I rarely attended ward activities. My involvement with the Church was limited to Church basketball, sacrament meetings, and most priesthood meetings. Then I met Carolyn.

Far more guys than girls attended the university, and at school dances, young ladies walking into the room typically never made it even halfway across the dance floor without being asked to dance. One night I saw a friend sitting down with four or five girls huddled around him. I approached and said jokingly, "Hey, this isn't fair. You're hoarding girls."

"Sit down," he said. "And if you can get anybody to accept, you're welcome to dance with any of these girls, except this blonde right here." He pointed to a girl sitting to his left. She laughed.

I sat down, and my friend introduced me to everybody in the group. Most of the girls were roommates; my friend had gone to high school with two of them. Carolyn was the blonde, the one who interested me most— probably because she was the one I was not supposed to be interested in! He had been joking, however, so we talked and danced. She had a unique personality, and she laughed easily. I liked her.

Carolyn and I started going out. The more Carolyn and I went out, the more I liked her. I began to see qualities in her that I admired and that I lacked, qualities like spiritual depth, strong faith, a solid testimony, and conviction.

Carolyn was more than active in Church and institute. In addition to being the Relief Society president of her campus ward, she was always involved in the planning of institute socials and activities. I started getting more involved with the Church because if I wanted to spend time with her, that is where she would be. The more I did things of a religious nature, the more interested she seemed to be in me.

One morning during our priesthood meeting, ward leaders asked for volunteers to do baptisms for the dead. I didn't have anything pressing that evening; Carolyn would be in meetings, so I volunteered.

On the evening that I was going to the temple, I got cleaned up and put on a suit and tie. "Where are you going all dressed up?" one of my roommates asked.

"I'm going to the temple to do baptisms for the dead," I replied.

Then he said something that made me cringe. "Ooh, won't Carolyn be proud!"

Evidently, if I had been made of glass, I couldn't have been any more transparent. I received an ugly little revelation about myself. I was a pretend-to-be-righteous, self-serving sham—a Pharisee wannabe. That may be a little overstated, but it was how I felt at that moment. My actions were positive, but my motives were questionable.

Had I been genuinely honest with myself, I would have admitted that I didn't care about the people who had died and were waiting for the saving ordinance of baptism. I wasn't thinking about helping them or my priesthood leaders or serving God by going to the temple. I was interested in making points with Carolyn. It wasn't baptisms for the dead—it was baptisms for the girlfriend.

On the way to the temple that night I felt chastened. I was ashamed of my self-serving attitude. I felt humbled. I prayed for forgiveness, and I decided that part of my repentance would be to never tell Carolyn that I had gone to the temple that night. I never did.

The temple experience was tremendous. I had only been baptized for the dead once before, and so many people had been participating on that occasion that I only got to be baptized for fourteen people. But that night, I was baptized and confirmed for more than 120 people. I left the temple waterlogged, exhausted, and uplifted. I thought about the people for whom I had received baptism and hoped that they would accept the ordinance offered to them.

Whether we are teaching the gospel, studying the scriptures, obeying the commandments, or serving in the Church, it is not only *what* we do that matters but also *how* and *why* we do it. Truly righteous acts come from truly righteous motives and desires.

I'm not saying that unless your motives are correct, you should not serve. I still do a lot of things because I am assigned to do them or feel an obligation. These are not the best motives, but they are not the worst. I used to do many things out of fear, so this is progress!

However, as we serve for whatever reason, if we allow the Spirit to work within us, we will begin to serve more often for the best reason: love for God and love for His children; we will serve with charity, which is the pure love of Christ.

In a conference address, Elder Oaks said, "When we think of service, we usually think of the acts of our hands. But the scriptures teach that the Lord looks to our thoughts as well as to our acts."[1] He then cited a commandment given to the children of Israel that they were to serve God with all of their heart and all of their soul (see Deuteronomy 11:13).

Elder Oaks also taught, "Latter-day revelation declares that the Lord requires not only the acts of the children of men, but 'the Lord requireth the heart and a willing mind'" (D&C 64:34).[2] Finally, Elder oaks listed six reasons a person might have for serving; this list could also be used as a reason for keeping the commandments or doing any of the other things that our Father in Heaven encourages us to do. In a countdown fashion, these are the reasons:

6. The hope for an earthly reward.
5. A personal desire to gain good companionship.
4. A fear of punishment.
3. A sense of duty or out of loyalty to friends or family or traditions.
2. The hope of an eternal reward.
1. Charity.

"If our service is to be most efficacious," Elder Oaks added, "it must be accomplished for the love of God and the love of His children."[3]

Doing the right thing for a less-than-perfect reason is always better than doing something wrong. But even if we are obedient, even if we serve faithfully, there might be room to repent by changing our attitude or improving our motives. As we mature spiritually, our motives will also mature. As our motivation becomes more pure, we will begin to better understand how and why the Lord Jesus Christ and our Father in Heaven continue to work to bring to pass the immortality and eternal life of man.

Notes
1. Dallin H. Oaks, "Why We Serve," *Ensign*, November 1984, 12.
2. Ibid.
3. Ibid., 13–14.

# 7
# Relying upon the Lord for Strength

WE ARE ALL AT different levels of spiritual strength and maturity in God's kingdom. Alma's counsel to his sons Helaman, Corianton, and Shiblon provides an insightful view of three different types of Church members, or three different conditions in which we might find ourselves.

Because Helaman turns out to be a mighty prophet of God, we might not realize that earlier in his life, he appears to have lacked commitment to the gospel. Worried about Helaman's undecided status, Alma shares with his son in great detail his own struggles with sin and the pain he experienced before he repented. He pleads with Helaman to avoid this painful type of experience by choosing to serve God and being faithful. Alma's words to Helaman include such phrases as, "Now you may suppose that this is foolishness in me" and "O, remember my son, and learn wisdom in thy youth; yea, learn in thy youth to keep the commandments of God" (Alma 37:6, 35).

In a later interview with Helaman, Alma asks, "Believest thou in Jesus Christ, who shall come?" Helaman responds that he believes everything his father had taught him. Alma then asks Helaman if he will keep "my commandments," to which Helaman replies, "I will keep thy command-ments with all my heart" (Alma 45:4, 6–7). Helaman had resolved to serve God and had become firm in that commitment. His strength and commit-ment came from his faith in Christ and his willingness to keep the com-mandments.

Corianton is the son with problems that are easiest to recognize. He was not steadfast in the faith, and he committed serious transgressions. Alma's words were designed to help Corianton recognize and take respon-sibility for his sins and to feel painful, yet appropriate, Spirit-inspired guilt. "I would not dwell upon your crimes, to harrow up your soul, if it were not for your good" (Alma 39:7).

Because of the seriousness of Corianton's transgressions, we may miss another of his weaknesses. Corianton's father tells him, "Now this is what I have against thee; thou didst go on unto boasting in *thy strength* and *thy wisdom*" (Alma 39:2; emphasis added). Corianton had either forgotten or had never recognized that God was the source of his strength and wisdom. He did not rely upon the Lord but put his trust in his own strength, which resulted in his downfall.

From all we can learn from the scriptures, Shiblon had always been solid in his testimony and never wavered in his obedience to the command-ments of God. What message can a parent give a child who is steadfast and faithful? Alma expresses the marvelous joy that he has already felt because of Shiblon's diligence. He manifests his confidence in Shiblon, telling him, "I trust that I shall have great joy in you, because of your steadiness and your faithfulness unto God; for as you have commenced in your youth to look to the Lord your God, even so I hope that you will continue in keeping his commandments" (Alma 38:2–3).

Alma also warns Shiblon about becoming complacent in his righteous efforts. Alma had witnessed Corianton boast of his strength and wisdom and he cautions Shiblon to beware of pride and self-righteousness. Alma tells his son to be patient with the people he is teaching and to love them. Because Shiblon has tremendous spiritual strength and wisdom, Alma reminds him that these things are gifts from God.

Helaman in his undecided condition; Corianton in his sinful state, having fallen off the path; and the valiant Shiblon all needed the power of Jesus Christ through His atoning sacrifice to be saved. As Alma reminds Shiblon, "There is no other way or means whereby man can be saved, only in and through Christ" (Alma 38:9).

Elder Dallin H. Oaks taught that Satan is not only aware of and trying to take advantage of our weaknesses but also that the adversary is also familiar with our strengths. According to Elder Oaks, "Satan can also attack us where we think we are strong—in the very areas where we are proud of our strengths. He will approach us through the greatest talents and spiritual gifts we possess. If we are not wary, Satan can cause our spiritual downfall by corrupting us through our strengths as well as by exploiting our weaknesses."[1]

Life in mortality can seem frightening when we learn that we have a constant enemy who attacks our weaknesses as well as our strengths. Moroni tells us that if we will humble ourselves before God and exercise faith in Him, then God will "make weak things become strong unto" us (Ether 12:27). However, if Satan can attack us even where we are strong, can we ever be safe? Is it possible that we can become so strong that the devil has no power over us? The answer is "no" and "yes."

No, a person cannot reach a condition during mortality where the possibility of sin does not exist. Agency allows us the opportunity to overcome as well as the risk of *being* overcome. "Wherefore, men are free according to the flesh; . . . free to choose liberty and eternal life, through the great Mediator of all men, or to choose captivity and death, according to the captivity and power of the devil" (2 Nephi 2:27).

Even those who have received the more sure word of prophecy are still capable of sinning. Elder Bruce R. McConkie taught the concept "that all men commit sin before and after baptism, and for that matter, before and after their calling and election is made sure, is self-evident. There has been only one Sinless One—the Lord Jesus who was God's own Son."[2]

Yes, we can overcome the temptations of the adversary through the grace of Jesus Christ and by relying upon the strength of the Spirit. We may not *be unshakable*, but with God's help we can live so that we *will not be shaken* from the faith. In other words, we are capable of sinning, but in the strength of God we refuse to sin. Jesus taught His disciples that "with men this is impossible; but with God all things are possible" (Matthew 19:26).

The Book of Mormon prophet Jacob writes about his confrontation with an anti-Christ named Sherem. Jacob tells us that Sherem was learned and "had a perfect knowledge of the language of the people; wherefore, he could use much flattery, and much power of speech, according to the power of the devil." Sherem sought out Jacob that he might debate him, hoping to shake Jacob from the faith (Jacob 7:4–5).

But Jacob said, "I truly had seen angels, and they had ministered unto me. And also, I had heard the voice of the Lord speaking unto me in very word from time to time; wherefore, *I could not be shaken*" (Jacob 7:5; emphasis added). Jacob demonstrates his unshakable testimony as he, with the help of the Lord, confounds Sherem on every point.

One year when I was teaching the Book of Mormon in seminary, I based the unofficial theme for my classes on Jacob's experience. The theme I chose was "developing an unshakable testimony." At the time, I believed that Jacob had reached a point in his spiritual maturity where he actually could not be shaken by anyone or anything. Now when I read Jacob's declaration that he could not be shaken, I think he was referring to that particular incident with Sherem. Although trying to make our testimonies unshakable is a worthy goal, I do not think that anyone can become completely unshakable while in mortality.

Some might use Job or Captain Moroni as examples of men who are so spiritually mature that they are unshakable. Again, it is not that they could not fall to temptation but simply that with the strength of the Spirit, they refused to be overcome.

Many Latter-day Saints have so much spiritual strength that they are not easily shaken, or at least they experience *moments* when they cannot be shaken. However, because of our fallen, mortal condition, the possibility of falling to the temptations of the adversary is a constant. Consider this statement by President Brigham Young:

> Do not suppose that we shall ever in the flesh be free from temptations to sin. Some suppose that they can in the flesh be sanctified, body and spirit, and become so pure that they will never again feel the effects of the power of the adversary of truth. Were it possible for a person to attain to this degree of perfection in the flesh, he could not die, neither remain in a world where sin predominates. Sin has entered into the world, and death by sin. I think we shall more or less feel the effects of sin so long as we live, and finally have to pass the ordeals of death.[3]

We might think that if anyone has reached a condition of being unshakable, it would be the prophets and the apostles. However, Wilford Woodruff asserted that "there never was a prophet in any age of the world but what the devil was continually at his elbow. This was the case with

Jesus himself. The devil followed him continually trying to draw him from his purposes and to prevent him carrying out the great word of God."[4]

Elder Clifford E. Young, an assistant to the Quorum of the Twelve, met with President Heber J. Grant a few weeks before President Grant passed away. During one meeting, Elder Young heard President Grant, a prophet of God, in the final weeks of his life pray, "O God, bless me that I shall not lose my testimony and keep faithful to the end!"[5]

Thomas B. Marsh was the first president of the Quorum of the Twelve in this dispensation. He apostatized and lost his membership in the Church while the Prophet Joseph was still alive. After the Saints moved west and established Salt Lake City, Marsh returned to the Church, seeking forgiveness. On September 6, 1857, Brigham Young introduced Brother Marsh to a congregation assembled in the Bowery and allowed him to speak.

In his remarks, Marsh admitted that he had become jealous of Joseph Smith, had lost the Spirit, and had became an apostate. He said that many had asked how a man in his position and with his experience could fall away. "I told them not to feel too secure, but to take heed lest they also should fall." Marsh said that it had not entered his mind "as to the possibility of men falling away."[6]

When Marsh concluded speaking, President Young stood and asked who was willing to accept Brother Marsh back into full fellowship. The congregation was unanimous in its vote to accept Brother Marsh back into the Church.

President Young recognized that even though Thomas B. Marsh had just warned the congregation that anyone could fall, Marsh himself stated that he would *never* leave the Church again. President Young said, "I presume that brother Marsh will take no offense if I talk a little about him."[7] He went on to talk about all that Brother Marsh had gone through and how his apostasy had affected him. He said:

> If [Marsh] had good sense and judgment, he would not have spoken as he has. He has just said, "I will be faithful, and I will be true to you." He has not wisdom enough to see that he has betrayed us once, and [doesn't] know but what he will again. He has told me that he would be faithful, and that he would do this and the other; but he [doesn't] know what he will do next week or next year.[8]

President Young may not have been the most tactful person in the world, but he taught a powerful truth to those assembled that day in the Bowery. After speaking of Marsh's lack of wisdom in telling people that he would never fall away again, President Young said of himself, "I do not know what I shall do next year; . . . You never heard me say that I was going to be true to my God; for I know too much of human weakness: but I pray God to preserve me from falling away—to preserve me in the truth."[9] The prophet of God explained to the Saints that he did not depend upon himself because he knew too much about human weakness to say that he would never fall. Brigham Young knew that his strength came from God.[10]

The spiritually mature are wise enough to know that they cannot put their trust in the arm of flesh (2 Nephi 4:34). They know that they will only become steadfast in the kingdom if they remain humble and seek God's strength. They are confident in themselves to the degree that they follow the Spirit. "I can do all things through Christ which strengtheneth me" (Philippians 4:13).

As we become firmer in the faith and more committed to keeping God's commandments with exactness, we must never forget that no matter how righteous we become, we cannot be saved in the kingdom of God without the grace of the Lord Jesus Christ. We cannot perfect ourselves. "God is my strength and power: and he maketh my way perfect" (1 Samuel 22:33).

After an extremely successful mission among the Lamanites, Ammon rejoiced as he recounted all that had been accomplished. His brother and fellow missionary Aaron chided him for what he thought was boastfulness and pride. But as pleased as Ammon was with their achievements and as confident as he was in his and his brothers' abilities to do the Lord's work, he recognized that it was the Lord's power and His great gifts to these missionaries that made them successful. Ammon responded to his brother, "I know that I am nothing; *as to my strength I am weak*; therefore I will not boast of myself, but I will boast of my God, for *in his strength I can do all things*" (Alma 26:12; emphasis added).

We all know people who have tried and failed many times to break bad habits or repent of sins that seemed too difficult for them to conquer. When they finally admitted to God in humble prayer that they were not strong enough to overcome their particular weaknesses and that without His help they would continue to fail, the strength that they lacked was supplied from a divine source. Through the grace of God, they became strong.

The Bible Dictionary, under *grace*, states that it is "through the grace of the Lord that individuals, through faith in the atonement of Jesus Christ and repentance of their sins, receive strength and assistance to do good works that they otherwise would not be able to maintain if left to their own means."[11] Grace is the power that enables us to return to our Father in Heaven and become like Him. As we mature spiritually, we gain a deeper appreciation for this power, and our strength increases as we rely upon the Lord.

Notes

1. Dallin H. Oaks, "Our Strengths Can Become Our Downfall," *Ensign*, October 1994, 12.
2. McConkie, *Doctrinal New Testament Commentary*, 3:342.
3. Brigham Young, in *Journal of Discourses*, 10:173.
4. Wilford Woodruff, in *Journal of Discourses*, 13:163.
5. As cited by John Longden, in Conference Report, October 1958, 70.
6. Thomas B. Marsh, in *Journal of Discourses*, 5:206.
7. Brigham Young, in *Journal of Discourses*, 5:209.
8. Ibid., 212.
9. Ibid., 212–13.
10. Ibid., 213.
11. Bible Dictionary, 697.

# 8

# Blessings and Gratitude

WE OFTEN TALK IN the Church about gaining the blessings of exaltation, becoming joint-heirs with Jesus Christ, and receiving all that the Father has. While it is important that we prepare ourselves during mortality to receive all the blessings promised in our future eternal existence, we should also be aware of the many blessings that can be ours during our mortal life on the earth. We may have to wait to receive *all* that the Father has and to experience a *fulness* of joy, but we don't have to wait for many of God's other blessings.

King Benjamin stated that God "doth require that ye should do as he hath commanded you; for which if ye do, *he doth immediately bless you*" (Mosiah 2:24; emphasis added). It does not sound like there is much waiting for those blessings. Later in the same chapter we are told to consider the happy state of those who keep God's commandments because "they are blessed in all things, both temporal and spiritual" (Mosiah 2:41).

A spiritually maturing person will seek for all of the blessings of God available in this life and be truly thankful for any blessings received. Sometimes people are troubled with the concept of seeking blessings. We are taught in the scriptures that coveting or seeking after signs is wrong. We are also told numerous times throughout the scriptures to knock, seek, and ask for wisdom, truth, and blessings. Paul even instructs us to "covet earnestly the best gifts" (1 Corinthians 12:31). Through the Prophet Joseph Smith, the Lord said, "Hearken and hear, O ye my people, saith the Lord and your God, ye whom I delight to bless with the greatest of all blessings" (D&C 41:1).

Speaking of the blessing of spiritual communication and personal revelation, President Young said, "I am satisfied, however, that in this respect, we live far beneath our privileges."[1] This is likely true of other blessings as well. Many of us do live far beneath our privileges, receiving far fewer blessings than those available to us. Why would this be the case?

I was introduced as "the local Mormon" to a woman in a predominantly non-LDS setting. She seemed thrilled to meet a Latter-day Saint and then explained to me why she was so impressed. Years earlier she had been in the hospital with what appeared to be a life-threatening condition. Several clergy had visited her, including her own minister. They prayed for her and comforted her, but her situation worsened, and she believed her time to die had arrived. One evening a couple of young men entered the hospital room and gave a blessing to the woman in the bed next to her. She felt something as she listened to the blessing, so after they had concluded and were about to leave, she said, "Could you give me a blessing too?"

"Well," she reported to me, "they did, and I started getting better from that very moment. Within a week, I was home, and a short time later, I had completely recovered." She concluded her story with this statement: "I found out that they were Mormon missionaries, and any time a member of my family gets sick, I call for the Mormon elders."

I asked her if she had ever had the missionaries visit her home to hear their message about the gospel. She replied, "No, I have my own religion. But if I get sick, I know who to call because I know who has the power to heal."

Here was a woman who had received a few blessings through the restored priesthood of God but lived far beneath her privileges of available blessings. What about those of us who are members of the Church? We have accepted the fulness of the gospel. Why would we, as President Young said, live beneath our privileges of receiving blessings from God? Here are a few possible reasons:

1. We are not aware of the blessings offered to us in this life, so we do not seek after them.

2. We do not live worthily to receive some blessings. Our lives are such that we cannot be blessed as much as our Father in Heaven would like to bless us. We do not keep the commandments that would bring us specific blessings. Doctrine and Covenants 130:20–21 states, "There is a law irrevocably decreed in heaven before the foundation of this world, upon which all blessings are predicated—And when we obtain any blessing from God, it is by obedience to that law upon which it is predicated."

3. Although we may be worthy of awesome blessings, Heavenly Father might withhold some of them as part of our earthly trial. In an October 1989 general conference address, Elder Richard G. Scott said that in addition to "yes" and "no" answers to our prayers, the Lord will sometimes respond "a third way to prayer by *withholding an answer* when the prayer is offered." Elder Scott said that the reason He does this "is to have us grow through faith in Him, obedience to His commandments, and a willingness to act on truth."[2] Like answers to prayers, blessings may be withheld to test our faith and to help our growth and spiritual development.

4. We may be receiving blessings that we do not recognize. A lack of maturity or sensitivity to the Spirit may result in our not being able to see the blessings we receive from God on a regular basis.

We can do something about each of the circumstances that hinder the receipt of blessings. Through scripture study and prayer, we can become aware of the blessings our Father in Heaven is willing to offer. We can pay the price through obedience and righteousness for greater spiritual blessings in this life because "when we obtain any blessing from God, it is by obedience to that law upon which it is predicated" (D&C 130:21).

We can faithfully endure and be patient when we do not receive specific blessings because our Heavenly Father, in His infinite wisdom, withholds temporal blessings for our eternal well-being. And we can become more sensitive to the Spirit and thereby recognize and appreciate the many blessings we constantly receive.

Not everyone is blessed with goodly parents. Not everyone is given the blessings of marriage and children in mortality, even when those blessings are the ones most desired. Perhaps we do have a spouse or children, but they are currently causing more heartache than joy. Many aspects of this life require us to be patient and exercise faith.

One of the greatest blessings that can come to a person who is not receiving the specific blessing that he desires is the blessing of peace. Peace that comes from the Spirit is a remarkable blessing that can make a seemingly unbearable situation bearable. In the midst of a long and brutal war, when part of the greatly outnumbered Nephite army had nearly starved to death, Helaman recounted that the Lord "did speak peace to our souls, and did grant unto us great faith, and did cause us that we should hope for our deliverance in him" (Alma 58:11).

During a moment of doubt when Oliver Cowdery sought a confirming witness that the things being restored through Joseph Smith were really from God, Oliver was reminded of a previous witness he had received. "If you desire a further witness, cast your mind upon the night that you cried unto me in your heart, that you might know concerning the truth of these things. Did I not speak peace to your mind concerning the matter?" (D&C 6:22–23).

Being comforted by the Holy Spirit is an often-overlooked blessing that can come to us in this life. "Peace I leave with you, my peace I give unto you: not as the world giveth, give I unto you. Let not your heart be troubled, neither let it be afraid" (John 14:27).

After sixteen years in one home, I moved my family to a new location in a different state. It was a hectic and stressful summer, which included preparing and selling our old home and purchasing a new home. Packing, moving, and settling into a new neighborhood, new ward, and new job were not easy. Add to that the extremely painful experience of the death of a loved one just before we moved.

One Sunday afternoon shortly after the move, my wife and I were talking about how difficult things had been the previous few months. She turned the conversation to how blessed we had been and began to specifically recall all the ways that we had been blessed—not only recently—but also throughout our lives. I was moved by her spirit of gratitude and added some of my own thoughts about how many blessings we had received.

For about two hours, we shared our feelings of gratitude as we counted our many blessings, naming them one by one. It was a very spiritual experience for me because I tend to focus on the negative aspects of life. However, an important part of receiving blessings from God and maturing spiritually is recognizing and being grateful for the blessings we have received. A true attitude of gratitude opens the windows of heaven even wider.

We need to count our blessings more often. Individually, as couples, and as families, we need to take time occasionally to remember all the many ways we have been blessed throughout our lives. Elder Henry B. Eyring once pointed out that if we count our blessings with faith, the Holy Ghost will often bring other blessings to mind.[3] As we do this, not only will we recognize that our Father in Heaven loves us and consistently blesses us, but we will also be filled with gratitude. Sincere feelings of gratitude bring the Spirit into our hearts.

Let us reflect on a few blessings. Consider the blessings of repentance, the commandments, the specific commandment of the Word of Wisdom, the patience of our Father in Heaven as He reveals to us our weaknesses, and the great blessing of spiritual gifts.

Isn't it an amazing thing that we can be forgiven for the stupid things we have done and for the sins we have committed? One of the most powerful phrases from the scriptures is, "He who has repented of his sins, the same is forgiven, and I, the Lord, remember them no more" (D&C 58:42). Because of the atoning sacrifice of the Lord Jesus Christ, I can have my slate wiped clean.

In Elder Bruce R. McConkie's first conference address as a member of the Quorum of the Twelve, he spoke of having faith in Christ and moving forward from where we are even if our past performance has not been stellar. He said, "Let this then be our covenant—*whatever the past has been*—let this then be our covenant, that we will walk in all the ordinances of the Lord blameless. Let this be our covenant, that we will keep the commandments of God and be living witnesses of the truth and divinity of this glorious work."[4]

Doctrine and Covenants 59:4 reads, "And they shall also be *crowned with blessings from above, yea, and with commandments not a few,* and with revelations in their time—they that are faithful and diligent before me" (emphasis added). The Lord tells us He is going to crown us with blessings and commandments not a few. Commandments truly are blessings of protection from the power of the adversary.

While obedience to the Word of Wisdom does not guarantee good health, it does contribute to our physical and spiritual health and to our happiness. Obedience to the Word of Wisdom also helps us know that, most likely, the specific health challenges that we do face are meant to be part of our life experiences and challenges.

Ether 12:27 tells us that if we come unto the Lord, He will show unto us our weakness. I believe that just as truth is revealed to us line upon line and precept upon precept, our specific areas of weakness are also revealed to us a little at a time as we become ready to change and improve. My guess is that we all have weaknesses and sins we are not even aware of! I am thankful that God does not reveal everything that is wrong with me all at once. That would be discouraging indeed. But if we are desirous to become more spiritual and Christlike, and if we are sensitive to the Spirit, our Father in Heaven will unveil our weaknesses to us, often through life's experiences.

As members of The Church of Jesus Christ of Latter-day Saints, we are blessed to have the gift of the Holy Ghost. With the reception of this gift comes gifts of the Spirit. President Marion G. Romney wrote, "The gifts of the Spirit are given by the power of the Holy Ghost. Without the gift of the Holy Ghost, the manifestations of his gifts may not be enjoyed."[5]

In his book *The Infinite Atonement,* Tad Calister wrote that the gift of the Holy Ghost is necessary for us to have the gifts of the Spirit:

> This is not to suggest that others do not have faith to be healed, or wisdom or love, for those qualities can be developed to some extent by the light of Christ, which illuminates every soul, and likewise by those manifestations of the Holy Ghost that may temporarily descend upon an unbaptized person. There are many good and honorable people outside Christ's church who demonstrate godlike virtues. But faith in its fullest and most enduring measure, that faith that moves mountains, stops the mouths of lions, and quenches the violence of fire; that wisdom that duplicates the mind and will of the Lord; and that charity that resembles the pure love of Christ—these and all other divine attributes in their grandest and consummate expression, in their full and unrestricted godlike proportions, come only through the gift of the Holy Ghost.[6]

The gifts of the Spirit listed in the scriptures are only a sample of the available gifts. Just because we cannot find a gift mentioned in the scriptures that we have doesn't mean that we don't have a gift. Those of us with less-evident gifts may find comfort in these words from Joseph Smith: "The greatest, the best, and the most useful gifts, would be known nothing about by an observer."[7]

Through study, prayer, patriarchal blessings, and even the help of loved ones, we can identify our gifts. Each person with the gift of the Holy Ghost has access to spiritual gifts. Elder Marvin J. Ashton wrote, "One of the greatest tragedies of life, it seems to me, is to describe oneself as having no talents or gifts. When, in disgust or discouragement, we allow ourselves to become despairing and depressed because of our self-appraisal, it is a sad day for us and a sad day in the eyes of God."[8]

Elder McConkie noted that in the fullest sense, the gifts of the Spirit "are infinite in number and endless in their manifestations."[9]

In my research I came across a number of quotes so similar in nature that they caught my attention. Each included the phrase "of all people," referring to the Latter-day Saints, and each focused on how blessed we are as a people. Here are a few:

Wilford Woodruff: "I feel myself that *of all people* under heaven that ever lived, the Latter-day Saints have the greatest cause to rejoice."[10]

Abraham H. Cannon: "We *of all people* upon the face of the earth should be filled with that love of God which cannot be overcome."[11]

John A Widtsoe: "*Of all people* in the world we should and can see most clearly in this dark, man-made chaos. We have the light."[12]

George Q. Cannon: "We *of all people* should be happy and joyful. When the clouds seem the darkest and most threatening, and as though the storm is ready to burst upon us with all its fury, we should be calm, serene and undisturbed."[13]

Wilford Woodruff: "I feel that *of all people* under heaven we ought to be the most grateful to our God; and that we ought to remember to keep our covenants, and humble ourselves before him, and labor with all our hearts."[14]

And Church leaders closer to our own time confirm this concept.

Howard W. Hunter: "*Of all people* on the face of the earth, Latter-day Saints, with the perspective given them by the gospel, ought to be happy and optimistic."[15]

Ezra Taft Benson: "*Of all people*, we as Latter-day Saints should be the most optimistic and the least pessimistic."[16]

Elder Bruce R. McConkie said, "You and I are the most blessed and favored people on the face of the earth."[17] And Harold B. Lee stated that we have been a most blessed people above all other people.[18] When we take the time and thought to count our blessings, we will find that it is difficult not to be filled with gratitude.

As we mature spiritually, we will recognize the many blessings we have received and feel a deep sense of gratitude. We can see the lack of spiritual maturity in the world all around us in the apparent ingratitude of many people. President Gordon B. Hinckley wrote:

> Our society is afflicted by a spirit of thoughtless arrogance unbecoming those who have been so magnificently blessed. How grateful we should be for the bounties we

enjoy. Absence of gratitude is the mark of the narrow, uneducated mind. It bespeaks of a lack of knowledge and the ignorance of self-sufficiency. It expresses itself in ugly egotism and frequently in wanton mischief. . . . Where there is appreciation, there is courtesy, there is concern for the rights and property of others. Without appreciation, there is arrogance and evil. Where there is gratitude, there is humility, as opposed to pride. How magnificently we are blessed! How thankful we ought to be![19]

President Hinckley also said, "Gratitude is of the very essence of worship—thanksgiving to the God of Heaven, who has given us all that we have that is good."[20]

Occasionally, a financially comfortable Latter-day Saint may comment that those who are not doing so well need to be more faithful or more diligent so that they too may be blessed. We must remember that blessings come in different forms, and the blessings of God are infinite in number and endless in their manifestations. We cannot and should not judge others because of their lack of financial or other temporal blessings. President Benson said, "That man is greatest and most blessed and joyful whose life most closely approaches the pattern of Christ. This has nothing to do with earthly wealth, power, or prestige. The only true test of greatness, blessedness, joyfulness is how close a life can come to being like the Master, Jesus Christ. He is the right way, the full truth, and the abundant life."[21]

We are a people most blessed. And we will continue to be greatly blessed if we will keep the commandments, recognize and give thanks for the blessings we have received, seek greater blessings that our Father in Heaven desires to give to us, and try to pattern our lives after the Master. President Hinckley said, "If we will live the gospel, if we will put our trust in God, our Eternal Father, if we will do what we are asked to do as members of the Church of Jesus Christ of Latter-day Saints, we will be the happiest and most blessed people on the face of the earth."[22]

Notes

1. Young, *Discourses of Brigham Young*, 32.
2. "Learning to Recognize Answers to Prayer," *Ensign*, November 1989, 31–32; emphasis in original.
3. Richard G. Scott, "Remembrance and Gratitude," *Ensign*, November 1989, 13.
4. Bruce R. McConkie, "'I Know that My Redeemer Lives,'" *Ensign*, October 1972; emphasis added.
5. Romney, *Look to God and Live: Discourses of Marion G. Romney*, 32.
6. Callister, *The Infinite Atonement*, 270.
7. Smith, *Teachings of the Prophet Joseph Smith*, 246.
8. Ashton, *The Measure of Our Hearts*, 16.
9. McConkie, *Mormon Doctrine*, 315.
10. *Collected Discourses*, 2:201; emphasis added.
11. Ibid., 4:427; emphasis added.
12. John A. Widtsoe, in Conference Report, April 1942, 32; emphasis added.
13. George Q. Cannon, in *Journal of Discourses*, 15:376; emphasis added.
14. Woodruff, *The Discourses of Wilford Woodruff*, 122; emphasis added.
15. Hunter, *The Teachings of Howard W. Hunter*, 268; emphasis added.
16. Benson, *The Teachings of Ezra Taft Benson*, 401; emphasis added.
17. Bruce R. McConkie, in Conference Report, October 1948, 26.
18. Lee, *The Teachings of Harold B. Lee*, 389.
19. Gordon B. Hinckley, "With All Thy Getting, Get Understanding," *Ensign*, August 1988, 2–3.
20. Hinckley, *Teachings of Gordon B. Hinckley*, 250.
21. Ezra Taft Benson, "Jesus Christ—Gifts and Expectations," *Ensign*, December 1988, 2.
22. "Excerpts from Recent Addresses of President Gordon B. Hinckley," *Ensign*, April 1996, 72.

# 9
# The Proper Balance

THE OLDER I GET the more clearly I see the need for balance in our lives—a balance of work and recreation, of physical and mental exertion, and of spiritual and temporal activity. We should have social interaction, but we also need personal time alone for thoughtful meditation. The Savior Himself lived a life of perfect balance as He "increased in wisdom and stature, and in favour with God and man" (Luke 2:52).

President Gordon B. Hinckley said that all of us have a fourfold responsibility to the Lord, to our families, to our employer, and to ourselves "to take some time to do a little meditating, to do a little exercise." Concerning this fourfold responsibility, President Hinckley observed:

> How do you balance them? I don't think that is difficult. I served in many capacities in this Church. I am the father of five children, who were young and growing up when I was serving in those various capacities. I think we had a good time and we took vacations together. We enjoyed life. We had family home evenings. We just did what the Church expected us to do. There is safety in that program;

it's inspired. . . . You have to sit down now and look at your resources. The major resource in this matter is time. I think you can do it. You balance it. You organize yourselves, as the Lord said, so that you can make that balance.[1]

We want our children to have opportunities that help them become balanced. While it is enjoyable to see them participate in sports, music, student government, academics, dance, drama, and school clubs, we must be careful that their spiritual growth is not neglected. Church classes, including seminary and institute, are helpful, but these classes cannot replace the spiritual teaching that should happen in the home. Elder M. Russell Ballard counseled parents to "be wise and do not involve children or yourselves in so many activities out of the home that you are so busy that the Spirit of the Lord cannot be recognized or felt in giving you the promised guidance for yourself and your family."[2]

Parents must help their children make wise decisions about involvement in things that may be good but are not necessary for salvation. Young people are not always spiritually mature enough to balance the use of their time. Elder Neal A. Maxwell warned:

> Ironically, inordinate attention, even to good things, can diminish our devotion to God. For instance, one can be too caught up in sports and the forms of body worship we see among us. One can reverence nature and yet neglect nature's God. One can have an exclusionary regard for good music and similarly with a worthy profession. In such circumstances, the "weightier matters" are often omitted. Only the Highest One can fully guide us as to the highest good which you and I can do.[3]

Although President Hinckley stated that he did not think it was that difficult to balance the things of life, many struggle with finding the right balance. In fact, Elder Maxwell said that "striking a proper balance is one of the keenest tests of our agency."[4] Whether we are helping our children or are working on our own lives, finding balance in life can be a challenging thing if we do not put our Father in Heaven first.

President Ezra Taft Benson taught that "when we put God first, all other things fall into their proper place or drop out of our lives."[5]

To find the appropriate balance in life, to prioritize properly so that our focus is on things of greatest worth, we must seek for divine guidance.

Elder Maxwell wrote:

> Therefore, we need to ask regularly for inspiration in the use of our time and in the making of our daily decisions. So often our hardest choices are between competing and desirable alternatives (each with righteous consequences), when there is not time to do both at once. Indeed, it is at the mortal intersections—where time and talent and opportunities meet—that priorities, like traffic lights, are sorely needed.[6]

Let us focus on a few areas where striking a proper balance is needed.

## SELF-CONFIDENCE AND HUMILITY

Some might view self-confidence and humility as incompatible characteristics. A worldly type of self-confidence consisting of pride and arrogance cannot coexist with humility. But there is a confidence borne of the Spirit that comes because of humility. Elder Marvin J. Ashton said, "How important it is in all our lives to develop an appropriate balance of confidence and humility. Proper self-confidence lets every man know there is a spark of divinity within waiting to be nurtured in meaningful growth."[7]

Speaking about the importance of humility, President Benson stated that humility is not weakness, nor does it mean "lack of courage, lack of faith, lack of self-confidence; but it means the recognition of a higher power upon which we are dependent."[8]

An institute instructor and friend named Dr. Rick Kent taught the difference between worldly and spiritual confidence in an understandable way. He noted that what a person needs more than self-confidence, self-esteem, or self-awareness is a spiritual awareness. To explain, he used the example of Moses in the first chapter of the Pearl of Great Price, where Moses "saw God face to face, and talked with him" (Moses 1:2). During this experience, three powerful messages were conveyed to Moses:

1. Moses was a son of God (see Moses 1:4).
2. God had a work for Moses to accomplish (see Moses 1:6).
3. Moses was in the similitude of the Only Begotten (see Moses 1:6).

Some modern psychologists might look at the statement made by Moses after his experience with the Lord and conclude that God had destroyed the self-esteem of Moses. He did say, "Now, for this cause I know that man is nothing, which thing I never had supposed" (Moses 1:10). Moses did not mean that man was nothing to God—we are His children; we are everything to Him. Moses was explaining his discovery that mortals are nothing in comparison to our Father in Heaven. He discovered that without God, man is nothing, but with God, man can accomplish anything.

When Moses was confronted and commanded by Satan to worship him, Moses replied, "I am a son of God, in the similitude of his Only Begotten; and where is thy glory that I should worship thee?" (Moses 1:13). Moses had developed a spiritual awareness. He was confident in himself because he was a follower of God, and he had total confidence in his Father.

The key to this balance of confidence and humility is the Spirit. When we see our weaknesses without the Spirit, we often suffer from feelings of low self-worth. When we see those same weaknesses with the Spirit, we are humbled and drawn closer to God as we seek strength to overcome our weaknesses. When we see our strengths without the Spirit, we tend to become arrogant and conceited. When we view those same strengths with the Spirit, we recognize that our gifts and talents were given to us by God, and we are humbled. Humility comes through the Spirit and provides balance.

## INTELLECTUAL AND SPIRITUAL DEVELOPMENT

Jacob, the younger brother of Nephi, tells us that "to be learned is good if they hearken unto the counsels of God" (2 Nephi 9:29). What happens if we become learned but do not listen to and follow the counsel of God? We not only cheat ourselves of greater learning, but we also unwittingly follow Satan's plan. Jacob also says, "O that cunning plan of the evil one! O the vainness, and the frailties, and the foolishness of men! When they are learned they think they are wise, and they hearken not unto the counsel of God, for they set it aside, supposing they know of themselves, wherefore, their wisdom is foolishness and it profiteth them not. And they shall perish" (2 Nephi 9:28).

Our society tries to ensure that we receive a secular education. We support public schools with our tax dollars, and by law, school is mandatory for children up to a certain age. However, it is up to the family and the individual to make sure that sufficient spiritual learning takes place. To neglect spiritual instruction can put us dangerously out of balance. President Spencer W. Kimball said, "It is quite understandable how budding intellectuals could become unbalanced when most receive many times as much secular study as religious training and when many receive no spiritual. It is our feeling that every student in every church should have religious training to balance the secular."[9]

Intellectualism without spirituality can manifest itself in criticism of doctrine, policies, Church history, and leaders. Sometimes self-proclaimed intellectuals lose their faith in God and leave the fold. Some will maintain their membership in the Church but will snipe, gripe, and fight against certain aspects of the Church privately and publicly, at times even promoting their own version of what they think Church doctrine should be. President Joseph F. Smith wrote:

> Among the Latter-day Saints, the preaching of false doctrines disguised as truths of the gospel, may be expected from people of two classes, and practically from these only; they are:
>
> First—The hopelessly ignorant, whose lack of intelligence is due to their indolence and sloth, who make but feeble effort, if indeed any at all, to better themselves by reading and study; those who are afflicted with a dread disease that may develop into an incurable malady—laziness.
>
> Second—The proud and self-vaunting ones, who read by the lamp of their own conceit; who interpret by rules of their own contriving; who have become a law unto themselves, and so pose as the sole judges of their own doings. More dangerously ignorant than the first.[10]

Our Father in Heaven, an exalted, glorified being who has knowledge of all things, sent us to earth so that we might become like Him. Certainly, His plan would embrace our increase of knowledge and wisdom. Responding to an accusation by a scholar that the Church is an enemy of intellectualism, President Hinckley responded:

> If he meant by intellectualism that branch of philosophy which teaches "the doctrine that knowledge is wholly or chiefly derived from pure reason" and that "reason is the final principle of reality," then, yes, we are opposed to so narrow an interpretation as applicable to religion. Such an interpretation excludes the power of the Holy Spirit in speaking to and through man. Of course we believe in the

cultivation of the mind . . . but the intellect is not the only source of knowledge.[11]

The scriptures admonish us to "seek learning, even by study and also by faith" (D&C 88:118; 109:7). We must balance our learning so that we do not become filled with information but devoid of the Spirit. Both heart and mind are involved in the process of developing spiritual maturity. To be learned *is* good *if* we hearken unto the counsels of God.

## THE DIFFERENCE BETWEEN FEELINGS OF THE SPIRIT AND EMOTION

People commonly become emotional when they feel the Spirit. People often cry when they share their testimonies of the gospel, and there is nothing wrong with this. Problems arise, however, if someone believes that the Spirit cannot be experienced *unless* there is a show of emotion.

In the Missionary Training Center, I was called to be leader of a group of missionaries called to serve in Japan. Each night we got together for a small devotional and group prayer. One evening a missionary from our group shared a very moving testimony. As we knelt in prayer, the Spirit was strong in the room and many tears were shed. I remember thinking, "This is the way a mission is supposed to be."

The following evening I expected the same thing to happen but was disappointed because there was joking and laughing as the missionaries entered the room. The devotional presented by one of the elders was light and even comical. When we knelt in prayer, there were no tears, and I was upset because we did not duplicate the experience of the previous evening. I expressed my disappointment to the group immediately following the prayer because I felt that, being the leader, it was my responsibility to call these elders to repentance.

As we returned to our rooms, one of the elders said he wanted to talk to me. At twenty-five, he was older than the rest of us who were almost all still in our teens. "Why were you upset tonight?" he asked.

"Because it was not as spiritual as it was last night," I replied. "As missionaries, we should be much more spiritual."

"Last night was unusual," he explained. "You can't force special spiritual moments. Also, just because an elder isn't crying does not mean that he isn't feeling the Spirit."

I said, "I didn't feel the Spirit tonight."

"Maybe that is because you were expecting something much bigger. Or maybe because you were angry, you could not feel the Spirit. The Spirit can be a lot more subtle than it was last night." He concluded by saying, "I didn't cry tonight; in fact, I laughed, but I still felt the Spirit."

What that elder taught me that evening was true. I was young and inexperienced with spiritual things, and perhaps had a touch of self-righteousness. President Howard W. Hunter said:

> I get concerned when it appears that strong emotion or free-flowing tears are equated with the presence of the Spirit. Certainly the Spirit of the Lord can bring strong emotional feelings, including tears, but that outward manifestation ought not be confused with the presence of the Spirit itself. I have watched a great many of my brethren over the years and we have shared some rare and unspeakable spiritual experiences together. Those experiences have all been different, each special in its own way, and such sacred moments may or may not be accompanied by tears. Very often they are, but sometimes they are accompanied by total silence. Other times they are accompanied by joy. Always they are accompanied by a great manifestation of the truth, of revelation to the heart.[12]

Young people in the Church are sometimes confused and need to be instructed in the difference between simple emotion and emotion brought on by the Spirit. It only complicates things when adults add to the problem by sharing emotional stories to elicit tears. One day as I was preparing a seminary lesson, I thought of a particular story that I might use near the end of the class. *This will really make them cry,* I thought. Then I caught myself and wondered, *Why would I share this story just to make my students cry?* The answer was when people cry, they often think they are feeling the Spirit. I was considering manipulating the emotions of my students.

Stories, experiences, and testimonies should be shared if they reinforce what we are trying to teach. The Spirit whispers what is and is not appropriate. Our goal should be to feel the Spirit and provide the proper environment so that others may feel the Spirit as well. If the Spirit brings out emotion, that is one thing, but purposeful emotionalism is counterfeit spirituality and is inappropriate.

## THE BALANCE OF GRACE AND WORKS

President Hunter noted that when we "understand the atoning sacrifice of the Master, we are approaching a spiritual maturity. I don't think spiritual maturity ever comes to us until we understand the true significance of the atoning sacrifice of the Master by which he gave his life that we might have life everlasting."[13] Part of understanding the Atonement is comprehending the mission of Jesus Christ, what He did for each of us, and what is required on our part to gain exaltation.

The balance of grace that the Savior offers us and the necessity of individual effort required has been an elusive doctrine for many through the years. By the time of the mortal ministry of Jesus, many Jewish religious leaders had become extremists in their understanding of being saved by obedience to the law of Moses. The law had been given to bring the Israelites to Christ and prepare them for a higher law. In a sense, they became so fanatically focused on the law that the law itself became the object of worship, supplanting in their minds the need for a savior.

Even after conversion to the fulness of the gospel restored by Jesus himself, some Jewish converts still felt a need to live the law of Moses and insisted that Gentile converts conform to the Mosaic law as well. It is from this vantage point that the Apostle Paul wrote, "For by grace are ye saved through faith; and that not of yourselves: *it is* the gift of God: Not of works, lest any man should boast" (Ephesians 2:8–9). If the Jewish Christians had been balanced in their understanding of grace and works, it is doubtful that Paul would have downplayed works as much as he did. He preached grace because at that time they were out of balance, leaning heavily toward works.

WORKS                              **GRACE**

As time passed and Christians were removed from the original Jewish converts and the law of Moses, the concept of salvation shifted. People who were not so focused on the law read Paul's writings and came to believe that works were not necessary at all. Because of the Great Apostasy, beliefs had shifted but were again out of balance.

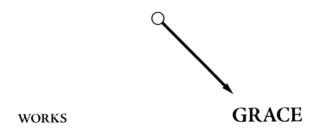

WORKS          **GRACE**

With the restoration of the gospel through the Prophet Joseph Smith, the balance of true doctrine was restored. We know that saving ordinances and righteous efforts on our part are necessary but are insufficient to save us. We cannot be saved without them, but even with them, we cannot be saved without the grace of Jesus Christ and His atoning sacrifice.

WORKS          **GRACE**

Our works are necessary but insufficient to save us without the grace of Christ.

This does not mean that our salvation comes half from our own works and half from the grace of Jesus Christ! The grace of Christ is far more important to our salvation than anything we could ever do, "for we know that it is by grace that we are saved, after all we can do" (2 Nephi 25:23). The above diagram is not to show that grace and works are of equal value to our salvation but to illustrate the needed balance of our understanding of grace and works.

Even with a correct perception of this doctrine, we may struggle to properly apply it in our lives. Many Latter-day Saints live righteously yet still have a constant fear that they are not doing enough. Elder Maxwell once said:

> Now may I speak, not to the slackers in the King-
> dom, but to those who carry their own load and more;
> not to those lulled into false security, but to those buf-
> feted by false insecurity, who, though laboring devotedly
> in the Kingdom, have recurring feelings of falling forever

short. . . . The first thing to be said of this feeling of inadequacy is that it is normal. There is no way the Church can honestly describe where we must yet go and what we must yet do without creating a sense of immense distance. Following celestial road signs while in telestial traffic jams is not easy, especially when we are not just moving next door—or even across town.[14]

Some people are out of balance because they are not relying enough on the atonement of Jesus Christ. They are thinking that somehow they must save themselves, even though that is clearly not possible.

On the other hand, some people do not put forth much effort to keep God's commandments, believing that Christ's grace will save them no matter how little they offer. In the mind of such an individual, the Atonement becomes a dodge for not having to live gospel principles. He might think, *I've been baptized, so I don't really need to try that hard because I am saved by grace and not by what I do, anyway.* These people are out of balance because they think that nothing is required of them.

A perfect scriptural example of the proper balance of grace and works is Nephi. We need to remember that Nephi did not write the first part of the Book of Mormon as a young man traveling through the wilderness. He fashioned the small plates and began engraving upon them thirty years after his family had left Jerusalem. He was writing after his experiences in the wilderness and crossing the ocean. By the time Nephi began writing on the small plates, he had already received revelations, witnessed miracles, beheld angels and visions, and seen the Lord. Nephi was a spiritually experienced prophet of God.

With this in mind, consider 2 Nephi 4. Nephi writes about the death of his father and mentions that a more historical, detailed record is on the large plates. Then, after stating the purpose of the small plates, he writes about his own personal dealings with the Lord through the years.

> Nevertheless, notwithstanding the great goodness of the Lord, in showing me his great and marvelous works, my heart exclaimeth: O wretched man that I am! Yea, my heart sorroweth because of my flesh; my soul grieveth because of mine iniquities.
>
> I am encompassed about, because of the temptations and the sins which do so easily beset me. And when I

desire to rejoice, my heart groaneth because of my sins. (2 Nephi 4:17–18)

Why does Nephi consider himself to be a wretched man? And how could his heart groan because of his sins? Nephi is an extremely righteous person, even a prophet of God.

I used to think that Nephi might be displaying false modesty or humility, and I felt like saying, "Come on, Nephi, how would you feel if you were like some of us? Walk in our shoes for a while and tell us how wretched you feel." But I have come to see that this was not false humility. Nephi knew that he was not perfect, and as he reflected on his life, he was sincerely humbled because of his weakness. With all that he had seen and experienced, he felt that he should have been better. This doesn't mean that Nephi had serious transgressions. In fact, Joseph Smith said that "the nearer man approaches perfection, the clearer are his views."[15] The more spiritual we become, the more clearly we perceive things, including our own weaknesses.

In Nephi's case, he had advanced so far spiritually that he saw all of his own small weaknesses and sins clearly, and he recognized how far he still was from becoming like Jesus. Again, feelings of inadequacy are common in a church where eventual perfection is an expectation. Nephi was troubled because of his imperfections, but he also recognized that the atonement of Christ was there for him—thus, helping him attain balance.

> And when I desire to rejoice, my heart groaneth because of my sins; *nevertheless, I know in whom I have trusted.*
>
> *My God hath been my support*; he hath led me through mine afflictions in the wilderness; and he hath preserved me upon the waters of the great deep.
>
> He hath filled me with his love, even unto the consuming of my flesh.
>
> He hath confounded mine enemies, unto the causing of them to quake before me.
>
> Behold, he hath heard my cry by day, and he hath given me knowledge by visions in the night–time.
>
> And by day have I waxed bold in mighty prayer before him; yea, my voice have I sent up on high; and angels came down and ministered unto me.

And upon the wings of his Spirit hath my body been carried away upon exceedingly high mountains. And mine eyes have beheld great things, yea, even too great for man; therefore I was bidden that I should not write them. (2 Nephi 4:19-25; emphasis added)

In the concluding verses of chapter 4, Nephi rejoices and says, "O Lord, I will praise thee forever; yea, my soul will rejoice in thee, my god, and the rock of my salvation," and "O Lord, I have trusted in thee, and I will trust in thee forever" (2 Nephi 4:30, 34). Nephi knows that his mortal life has not been and would not be perfect. But he also knows that because of his faithfulness and loyalty to the Savior and because of his sincere efforts to do the will of God, Jesus Christ would save him.

Here is an analogy to better understand what the Savior does for us and what we must do ourselves to be saved in the kingdom of God. Picture yourself onboard a large ship in the middle of the ocean. As you lean over the railing to look at something, you fall overboard. There you are in the cold, choppy water with the ship leaving you behind. A man standing on the deck calls to you and throws you a life preserver tied to a rope. All of us would know what to do in this circumstance. We would try to get to that life preserver so that we could be pulled to safety.

If the ocean represents our fallen condition, the man on the deck symbolizes Christ, and the life preserver is His saving grace through the Atonement, we would certainly do all we could to get to the life preserver that has been offered to us. However, some people believe that in order to be saved—to be worthy to be saved—they must swim to the ship, climb up the side, pull themselves over the railing and then, at Jesus' feet, say to Him, "Now I am worthy to be saved." That, by the way, is impossible!

You cannot say, "Don't fall overboard" because we are already in the deep. So what is our responsibility? Recognize the dire situation we are in and acknowledge that we cannot save ourselves. Admit that we need to be saved and that there is only one person who can save us. Look to the Savior; make our way to the life preserver He has offered us. Get into that life preserver and hang on tight. We must cling to that eternal lifeline as the Savior pulls us in, putting forth whatever effort we can to propel us closer to Him.

## THE BALANCE OF THE SPIRITUAL
## AND THE SECULAR

In addition to finding a balance of spiritual and secular in learning, we must balance the spiritual and secular in our daily lives. We have been talking about balance, but we cannot be too spiritual or too righteous. The biblical definition of pure, undefiled religion recorded by James is "to visit the fatherless and widows in their affliction, *and* to keep himself unspotted from the world" (James 1:27; emphasis added). Elder Carlos E. Asay said that, based on this definition, "the answer to the question ['Can a man or woman be too religious or too righteous?'] is an emphatic no. To say otherwise is to say that a man or woman can become too Christlike."[16]

The key to spiritual and secular balance is to avoid becoming a religious fanatic. In 1978, Church Educational System personnel were instructed by Elder Hinckley to grow with balance. He warned those who teach the gospel for a living not to make the gospel their only interest. He suggested reading secular history, literature, and the writings of contemporary thinkers. Elder Hinckley counseled religious educators to keep balance in their lives. "Beware of obsession. Beware of narrowness. Let your interests range over many good fields while working with growing strength in the field of your own profession."[17] All Church members can benefit from this sound advice.

Elder Bruce R. McConkie cautioned to stay in the mainstream of the Church and avoid fanaticism. "You don't have to live a life that's truer than true. You don't have to have an excessive zeal that becomes fanatical and becomes unbalancing."[18]

## CONCLUSION

Balance is a key to spiritual maturity. Elder Maxwell taught that "the narrowness of the straight and narrow way involves achieving a balance between tugging yet correct principles. . . . Balance on the straight and narrow path is crucial."[19] We must stay in the center of the path, being careful not to become a "fringite," avoiding gospel hobbies or extremism in any of the doctrines. As Elder McConkie counseled, "We would do well to have a sane, rounded, and balanced approach to the whole gospel and all of its doctrines."[20]

Notes

1. Hinckley, *Teachings of Gordon B. Hinckley*, 33–34.
2. M. Russell Ballard, "What Matters Most Is What Lasts Longest," *Ensign*, November 2005, 43.

3. Neal A. Maxwell, "Consecrate Thy Performance," *Ensign,* May 2002, 37.

4. Maxwell, *Notwithstanding My Weakness,* 5.

5. Ezra Taft Benson, "The Great Commandment—Love the Lord," *Ensign,* May 1988, 4.

6. Maxwell, *Notwithstanding My Weakness,* 5.

7. Marvin J. Ashton, "Who's Losing?" *Ensign,* November 1974, 41.

8. Benson, *The Teachings of Ezra Taft Benson,* 159.

9. Kimball, *The Teachings of Spencer W. Kimball,* 387.

10. Smith, *Gospel Doctrine,* 373.

11. Hinckley, *Teachings of Gordon B. Hinckley,* 301.

12. Howard W. Hunter, "Eternal Investments," address given to Church Educational System educators, February 10, 1989, 3.

13. Hunter, *The Teachings of Howard W. Hunter,* 7.

14. Neal A. Maxwell, "Notwithstanding My Weakness," *Ensign,* November 1976, 12.

15. Smith, *Teachings of the Prophet Joseph Smith,* 51. Moving toward exaltation could be likened to walking up a path strewn with large and small rocks, representing our sins and weaknesses. Sometimes the boulders that loom so large in front of us keep us from seeing the many smaller rocks that lie beyond the larger boulders. As we push aside the large rocks through repentance, we can see other stones or problems that we did not recognize before. As we walk up the path and get closer to God, the more clearly we can see all of our imperfections. Nephi, a great prophet, has no boulders on his path, but he sees all the little things he has not yet overcome. It is as if he were on a pathway scattered with gravel, and he is troubled that there are still pebbles on his path.

16. Carlos E. Asay, *In the Lord's Service: A Guide to Spiritual Development,* 49.

17. Gordon B. Hinckley, "Four Imperatives for Religious Educators," Church Educational System address, September 15, 1978, 3.

18. Bruce R. McConkie, "The Probationary Test of Mortality," address given at the Salt Lake Institute, January 10, 1982, 11.

19. Maxwell, *That Ye May Believe,* 138.

20. McConkie, *Doctrines of the Restoration,* 232.

# 10
# Seeking the Spirit

HOW IMPORTANT TO OUR personal progress in mortality is having the Spirit? In 1847, just a few months before Brigham Young led the first group of Saints to the Salt Lake Valley, the Prophet Joseph Smith appeared to him in a dream. President Young recorded the dream, saying:

> Joseph stepped toward me, and, looking very earnestly, yet pleasantly, said, "Tell the people to be humble and faithful, and be sure to keep the Spirit of the Lord, and it will lead them right. Be careful and not turn away the still, small voice, it will teach them what to do and where to go; it will yield the fruits of the kingdom. Tell the brethren to keep their hearts open to conviction, so that when the Holy Ghost comes to them their hearts will be ready to receive it. They can distinguish the Spirit of the Lord from all other spirits: it will whisper peace and joy to their souls: it will take malice, hatred, strife and all evil from their hearts, and their whole desire will be to do good, bring forth righteousness, and build up the kingdom of God. Tell the brethren if they

will follow the Spirit of the Lord they will go right. Be sure to tell the people to keep the Spirit of the Lord, and if they will, they will find themselves just as they were organized by our Father in heaven before they came, into the world. Our Father in Heaven organized the human family but they are all disorganized and in great confusion. . . ." Joseph again said, "Tell the people to be sure to keep the Spirit of the Lord, and to follow it, and it will lead them just right."[1]

Notice how many times Brigham Young was instructed and encouraged to make sure that his people had the Spirit of the Lord with them. What makes this encounter even more fascinating is that Wilford Woodruff had a similar experience. Although the messenger was different (President Young appeared to President Woodruff), the message was essentially the same. In the April 1944 general conference, Elder Marion G. Romney related the incident:

> In 1879, two years after the Prophet Brigham Young had died, President Wilford Woodruff was down in the mountains of Arizona traveling with Lot Smith. On one occasion, he had a vision or a dream in which he saw Brigham Young and Orson Hyde, and he asked Brigham Young if he would not come with him to Arizona and speak to the people. Brigham Young answered that he had done his talking in the flesh and that work was now left for Elder Woodruff and others to do. In his diary, President Woodruff quotes President Young as saying: "Tell the people to get the spirit of the Lord and keep it with them."[2]

Clearly one of the most important things a person can do to become spiritually mature is to seek the Spirit and enjoy its constant companionship. Like many of you, I have spent much of my life trying to avoid things that would drive the Spirit away. Perhaps it would be better if we would focus on getting and keeping the Spirit rather than staying away from situations and circumstances where the Spirit would depart from us. This may be a subtle difference, but if our focus is on doing things that invite the Spirit into our lives and that maintain our spirituality, we won't likely worry as much about things that cause us to lose the Spirit.

How can we receive and keep the Spirit when we are surrounded by things that are not spiritual? We live in a fallen world; the things of this world are telestial. We ourselves are telestial in nature. Our natural condition in this world is fallen because we have inherited a fallen body, a fallen mind, and a fallen nature. Yet our Father in Heaven does not want us to remain in this fallen state.

In a letter to the Saints in Corinth, Paul wrote, "But the natural man receiveth not the things of the Spirit of God: for they are foolishness unto him: neither can he know them, because they are spiritually discerned" (1 Corinthians 2:14). In the Book of Mormon, King Benjamin taught his people that "the natural man is an enemy to God" (Mosiah 3:19).

For years I was troubled by this statement. I did not want God to be my enemy while I struggled in mortality. I reasoned that our Father in Heaven loves His children and is not their enemy. Looking closer, I noticed that the scripture does not say that God is an enemy to the natural man but that the natural man is an enemy to God. As Elder Neal A. Maxwell noted, "The more we understand the virtues and attributes of God, the more we see that the ways of the natural man and woman have no place in heaven."[3]

If I remain in my fallen state, then I am at odds with my Heavenly Father. Not only am I fighting against Him, but I am also fighting against His plan for me to return to Him and become like Him. Fighting against God's tremendous plan of happiness is fighting against my own happiness. A person who refuses to follow God's plan is, in a sense, saying, "I don't want to be happy. I would rather do things my own way and be miserable than follow the plan my Father has provided and receive a fulness of joy."

King Benjamin observed that the natural man will be an enemy to God forever unless he yields to the Holy Spirit, puts off the natural man, and becomes a Saint through the atoning sacrifice of Christ. How do we put off the natural man and become spiritual in nature? Acting alone, no one can do this. The atonement of Christ and His grace make it possible for us to change. The Spirit acts as a catalyst to help us make necessary changes.

What is our part in this process? We must have the desire to overcome our weaknesses, sins, and fallen nature. We must humble ourselves and seek the help of God in recognizing where we need to change. "If men come unto me I will show unto them their weakness" (Ether 12:27). We must seek to have the Spirit with us and then follow the guidance given through that Spirit. Nephi taught, "Receive the Holy Ghost, it will show unto you all things what ye should do" (2 Nephi 32:5).

How do we seek for the Spirit in our life? What can we do that would invite the Spirit to dwell with us? Elder Dieter F. Uchtdorf taught that the doctrine and principles of the gospel never change, and "living according to the basic gospel principles will bring power, strength, and spiritual self-reliance into the lives of all Latter-day Saints."[4]

Studying the scriptures, praying, keeping the commandments, and attending church meetings are basic principles of living the gospel and have become known as Sunday School answers. Occasionally, I hear teachers ask a question and then add, "And I don't want to hear the Sunday school answers." I understand that students sometimes give the Sunday School answers if they haven't been paying attention because they figure they have a good chance of answering the unheard question correctly. However, these basics truly are the right answer to those seeking the Spirit.

If I want the Spirit with me, I need to study the scriptures regularly, sincerely striving to see and understand God's instructions to me. I do need to pray several times each day. My prayers need to be heartfelt and accompanied by thoughtful meditation and sometimes with fasting. I need to be obedient, keeping the commandments of God to the best of my ability and having a sincere desire to become even more obedient. I need to attend my church meetings—and not only attend but also earnestly worship. I need to accept and magnify callings. When possible, I need to attend and participate in temple ordinances regularly. And let me add one more Sunday School answer: Service is vitally important in preparing us to receive the Spirit of the Lord.

My father-in-law shared an experience with me. He was seeking an answer to an important question and had decided that he would spend the entire Sabbath preparing himself to receive the answer to his question through personal revelation. He was the high priests group leader in his ward at the time and had an early-morning meeting prior to the three-hour block of regular Church meetings. He began a fast on Saturday evening, planning to come home from Church and spend the rest of the day studying the scriptures in fasting and prayer.

During the early-morning priesthood leadership meeting, the bishop gave him several assignments that needed to be accomplished that afternoon. After completing those tasks, my father-in-law was contacted by a member of the high priests group who was going through a difficult time and needed to talk. Consequently, my father-in-law spent several hours with this brother. Shortly after that, my father-in-law was called upon to administer to two people in the ward who were sick. One of the people who was sick had scheduled his home teaching for that evening, so my father-in-law went with the sick man's companion to do his home teaching.

When he got home later that evening, although happy to be of service, he felt disappointed that he been unable to study the scriptures or spend time in prayer. Kneeling at his bed that night he prayed, expressing to God what he had planned to do and promising that the next opportunity he had to spend the day in fasting, prayer, and scripture study, he would do so because he still needed the answer to his particular challenge.

"I crawled into bed and was just drifting off to sleep," he told me, "when the answer to my question came clearly and powerfully to my mind. I got out of bed and got on my knees and thanked Heavenly Father for the knowledge He had given me. But I was somewhat confused. I had not spent the day studying and praying and preparing my mind to receive personal revelation. How had it come without the typical efforts of preparation?" As he wondered about this, these words came into my father-in-law's mind: "Service is blessings bought and paid for."

Our Father in Heaven had responded to my father-in-law's needs because my father-in-law had responded to the needs of our Father's children. Service is the sometimes-neglected Sunday School answer to the question, "How can I obtain the Spirit in my life?"

Each week when we attend sacrament meeting, we have the opportunity to partake of the sacrament, the ordinance that, according to Elder Vaughn J. Featherstone, ties more directly to the Atonement than any other.[5] If we listen closely to the sacrament prayers, we learn that by taking upon us the name of Christ, always remembering Him, and keeping the commandments He has given us, we can have His Spirit to be with us. Taking upon us His name is more than simply being baptized. When we agree to take upon us His name, we also agree to try to become like Him and to strive to have His image in our countenances.

I have designed a little quiz to help me evaluate where I am in the process of developing spiritual maturity. This quiz was never intended to be comprehensive; many more questions could be added. But these twenty basic questions can help us see where we are spiritually, what direction we are heading, or what we might need to be doing in our own personal progression.

# SPIRITUAL MATURITY QUIZ

1. Have you ever read the entire Book of Mormon?
2. Have you received a personal witness by the Spirit of the truthfulness of the gospel of Jesus Christ?
3. Do you have daily personal prayer?
4. Do you study the scriptures daily? (I've heard it said that if life is a test, we ought to make it an open-book test!)
5. Do you live worthy of having a temple recommend?
6. Do you attend the temple regularly?
7. Do you obey the commandments to the best of your ability?
8. Have you ever fasted for a full twenty-four hours without food or liquid?
9. Do you magnify your Church callings, including that of home teacher or visiting teacher?
10. Do you have regular family home evening?
11. Are you more interested in receiving the Lord's approval than you are in earning the praise, wealth, and glory of the world?
12. Do you avoid contention, harsh feelings, and anger?
13. Do you resist being critical of others, especially family members and those in authority?
14. Do you keep your mind and actions clean and pure?
15. Is your language appropriate for a person who has made a covenant with God?
16. Do you faithfully keep the Word of Wisdom?
17. Have you truly repented of your sins?
18. Do you serve others?
19. Do you love your family? Are you faithful to your spouse, both physically and emotionally?
20. Do you receive promptings from the Spirit? And do you *follow* those promptings?

The path that leads to spiritual maturity is the passageway by which we become like our Father in Heaven and His Son, Jesus Christ. It is the process of overcoming the world and developing Christlike qualities and characteristics, attributes that we have inherited from our Heavenly Father but only in their embryonic state. These qualities must be cultivated and amplified, which can only be accomplished with the aid of the Holy Spirit. Parley P. Pratt wrote:

An intelligent being, in the image of God, possesses every organ, attribute, sense, sympathy, affection, of will, wisdom, love, power and gift, which is possessed by God himself. But these are possessed by man in his rudimental state in a subordinate sense of the word. Or, in other words, these attributes are in embryo, and are to be gradually developed. They resemble a bud, a germ, which gradually develops into bloom, and then, by progress, produces the mature fruit after its own kind. The gift of the Holy Spirit adapts itself to all these organs or attributes. It quickens all the intellectual faculties, increases, enlarges, expands, and purifies all the natural passions and affections, and adapts them by the gift of wisdom to their lawful use. It inspires, develops, cultivates, and matures all the fine-toned sympathies, joys, tastes, kindred feelings, and affections of our nature. It inspires virtue, kindness, goodness, tenderness, gentleness, and charity. It develops beauty of person, form and features. It tends to health, vigor, animation, and social feeling. It develops and invigorates all the faculties of the physical and intellectual man. It strengthens, invigorates, and gives tone to the nerves. In short, it is, as it were, marrow to the bone, joy to the heart, light to the eyes, music to the ears, and life to the whole being.[6]

I love the following quote by Heber C. Kimball because it not only gives us an insight into the personality of our Father in Heaven, but it also helps us understand what the influence of the Spirit can mean in our own lives. Elder Kimball said:

I am perfectly satisfied that my Father and my God is a cheerful, pleasant, lively, and good-natured Being. Why? Because I am cheerful, pleasant, lively, and good-natured when I have His Spirit. That is one reason why I know; and another is—the Lord said, through Joseph Smith, "I delight in a glad heart and a cheerful countenance." That arises from the perfection of His attributes; He is a jovial, lively person, and a beautiful man.[7]

Just as Paul taught that the things of the Spirit can only be discerned by the Spirit, it is also true that the characteristics of God can only be developed through the Holy Spirit. One of the most vital aspects of maturing spiritually is having the Spirit with us. We can have the Spirit as a constant companion if our desires are sincere and our efforts are consistent. "And blessed are all they who do hunger and thirst after righteousness, for they shall be filled with the Holy Ghost" (3 Nephi 12:6).

Notes
1. Young, *Manuscript History of Brigham Young 1846–1847,* 529–30.
2. Marion G. Romney, in Conference Report, April 1944, 140.
3. Neal A. Maxwell, *Men and Women of Christ,* 124.
4. Dieter F. Uchtdorf, "Christlike Attributes—The Wind Beneath Our Wings," *Ensign,* November 2005, 100.
5. "Righteous Young Men Are Models against Evil," *Church News,* November 4, 1989, 10.
6. Pratt, *Key to the Science of Theology/A Voice of Warning,* 61.
7. Heber C. Kimball, in *Journal of Discourses,* 4:222.

# 11
# Handling Adversity Well

YEARS AGO, A FRIEND shared a scripture insight with me. He had me look at 1 Nephi 16:16, which reads: "And we did follow the directions of the ball, which led us in the more fertile parts of the wilderness." He then explained that Lehi and his family left the comfort of their home at Jerusalem and traveled through the wilderness to get to the promised land. There was no route available other than through the wilderness; however, when Lehi and his family followed the directions on the Liahona, they were led through the "more fertile parts of the wilderness." In other words, they were able to avoid the worse parts of the wilderness because they were guided by the Lord.

My friend likened Lehi's journey to our own journey through mortality. He explained that we leave the comforts and peace of our Heavenly home and travel to earth. Mortality is the wilderness we must pass through to reach our promised land of exaltation. But even though we must pass through the wilderness, if we follow the directions of our own Liahona—the scriptures, the teachings of the living prophets, the commandments, and the guidance from the Holy Ghost—we will be led through the "more fertile parts" of our wilderness.

Many negative and difficult things exist in our fallen world that we can avoid if we obey instructions from God. Speaking about the types of adversity we might face during mortality, Elder Richard G. Scott said:

> Trials, disappointments, sadness, and heartache come to us from two basically different sources. Those who transgress the laws of God will always have those challenges. The other reason for adversity is to accomplish the Lord's own purposes in our life that we may receive the refinement that comes from testing. It is vitally important for each of us to identify from which of these two sources come our trials and challenges, for the corrective action is very different.[1]

Although it is impossible to escape from all adversity during our mortal existence, we can avoid adversity that results from not keeping the commandments of God. Each person who lives on this earth will suffer setbacks, failures, disappointments, losses, trials, hurts, and deaths. President Gordon B. Hinckley said, "There is something of a tendency among us to think that everything must be lovely and rosy and beautiful without realizing that even adversity has some sweet uses."[2]

Adversity can strengthen us and help us become more pure, more holy. However, it is not simply going through adversity that makes a person strong. After all, if adversity made people stronger and better, everyone would be strong and good because everyone goes through adversity. It is not so much what a person experiences in this life as how that person handles those difficulties that matters.

Consider Nephi and Laman as case studies. Both left a comfortable home near Jerusalem; both sacrificed things left at home; both traveled through the wilderness, experiencing hunger, thirst, and fatigue; both felt the heat of the day and the cold of the night. Nephi and Laman trudged over the same paths and experienced similar hardships during their wilderness trek. Yet Laman came out of that experience a bitter, faithless, wicked individual, while Nephi emerged as a prophet of God.

Each of us has likely asked for painful experiences to be removed. We are in good company. Paul tells us that he suffered from some "thorn in the flesh" that he had asked God three times to remove (2 Corinthians 12:7–8).

Apparently, it was Heavenly Father's will that the problem remain. In the Garden of Gethsemane, the Savior Himself asked His Father, "If thou be willing, remove this cup from me: nevertheless not my will, but thine, be done" (Luke 22:42). The key to handling adversity well is humility, seeking to do the will of the Father rather than our own will.

What if all our prayers were answered according to our imperfect will rather than God's omniscient will? President Spencer W. Kimball shared this sobering insight:

> The power of the priesthood is limitless, but God has wisely placed upon each of us certain limitations. I may develop priesthood power as I perfect my life. I am grateful that even through the priesthood I cannot heal all the sick. I might heal people who should die. I might relieve people of suffering who should suffer. I fear I would frustrate the purposes of God.
>
> Had I limitless power, and yet limited vision and understanding, I might have saved Abinadi from the flames of fire when he was burned at the stake, and in doing so I might have irreparably damaged him and limited him to a lower kingdom. He died a martyr and went to a martyr's reward—exaltation. He would have lived on the earth and could have lost his faith, his courage, even his virtue, and his exaltation.
>
> I would likely have protected Paul against his woes if my power were boundless. I would surely have healed his "thorn in the flesh." And in doing so I might have foiled the program and relegated him to lower glories. Thrice he offered prayers, asking the Lord to remove the "thorn" from him, but the Lord did not so answer his prayers. Paul many times could have lost himself if he had been eloquent, well, handsome, and free from the things which made him humble.
>
> I fear that had I been in Carthage Jail on June 27, 1844, I might have deflected the bullets which pierced the bodies of the Prophet and the Patriarch. I might have saved them from the sufferings and agony, but lost to them the martyr's death and reward. I am glad I did not have to make that decision.

With such uncontrolled power, I surely would have felt to protect Christ from the insults, the thorny crown, the indignities in the court, physical injuries. Perhaps I would have struck down his persecutors with shafts of lightning. When he hung on the cross I would have rescued him and would have administered to his wounds and healed them, giving him cooling water instead of vinegar. I might have saved him from death and lost to the world an atoning sacrifice and frustrated the whole program.

Would you dare to take the responsibility of bringing back to life your own loved ones? I, myself, would hesitate to do so. I am grateful that we may always pray: "Thy will be done in all things, for thou knowest what is best."[3]

According to President John Taylor, the Prophet Joseph Smith said that God "would feel after their [the Saints'] heartstrings and try them in every way possible for them to be tried."[4] Commenting on President Taylor's statement, Elder Neal A. Maxwell said, "If our hearts are set too much upon the things of this world, they may need to be wrenched, or broken, or undergo a mighty change."[5]

Some might ask, "Why would a loving Father in Heaven not only allow us to go through painful experiences but also insist that we do?" Consider the purpose of life. Our goal is not only to return to our Father in Heaven to dwell with Him *and* to become like Him. A loving God would not remove something from His children that would help them return to Him. We might cry, "Please take away my pain and my sorrow!" But if, in His infinite wisdom, our Heavenly Father knows that we are experiencing the very challenge we need to gain exaltation, God will not remove that trial. He loves us too much to withdraw the things that would lead us back to His heart and home and to our eternal joy.

As parents we see our children going through difficult and painful situations, but we know when to step in and when not to interfere. If I were to protect my children from all negative experiences—being there at recess to make sure my son is not chosen last for kickball, ensuring that my daughter has a date to the prom, helping my children with exams at school, making sure nothing cruel is ever said to them—then my children would not learn the things they need to mature. In fact, if I kept them too sheltered, they wouldn't even be able to function in life.

Elder Scott points out:

> A fundamental purpose of earth life is personal growth and attainment. Consequently, there must be times of trial and quandary to provide opportunity for that development. What child could ever grow to be self-supporting in maturity were all the critical decisions made by parents? So it is with our Heavenly Father. His plan of happiness is conceived so that we will have challenges, even difficulties, where decisions of great importance must be made so that we can grow, develop, and succeed in this mortal probation.[6]

Good, loving parents want what is best for their children. Our Father in Heaven is a perfect parent. He has all wisdom and knowledge, including foreknowledge about each of us. God's love for His children is perfect and selfless, and His work and His glory are "to bring to pass the immortality and eternal life" of His children (Moses 1:39). Elder Scott added, "To get you from where you are to where He wants you to be requires a lot of stretching, and that generally entails discomfort and pain."[7] Another statement from that same conference address is very comforting: "Your Father in Heaven and His Beloved Son love you perfectly. They would not require you to experience a moment more of difficulty than is absolutely needed for your personal benefit, or for that of those you love."[8]

Spiritual maturity is developed when we avoid needless adversity through obedience to gospel principles and commandments and when we face the unavoidable adversities of life with faith, hope, and patience. This is not an easy task. It is difficult to see the positive aspects of adversity when we are in the midst of trials and tribulations. It takes great spiritual maturity to appreciate the worth of life's challenges while going through them.

When my sister Sharon was a junior in high school, she made the drill team. During one of the early practice sessions, her drill team instructor told her to stand up straight. When Sharon replied that she *was* standing straight, the instructor sent a note home suggesting that Sharon go to the doctor to see if one leg was shorter than the other or if there was some other problem.

We discovered that my sister had spinal scoliosis, or curvature of the spine. Our family doctor sent her to a specialist, who determined that the curvature was not too severe and that because Sharon had already experienced most of her growth, it probably would not get any worse. He explained that it should not cause any pain and it wasn't really noticeable, so she could just live with it. The specialist also taught my parents how to check for spinal scoliosis.

When they got home and were telling the rest of the family about the situation, Mom said, "Rich, let me show you how they check for scoliosis. They have you bend over and touch your toes . . ."

I bent over and tried to touch my toes.

"And if your spine is straight, both sides of the back are even, but if the spine is crooked, one side will be higher than the other . . . like yours."

The following week, I was off to see the specialist. Sure enough, I also had scoliosis. Mine was a little worse than Sharon's, and since I still had much of my growing to do, it was potentially a lot worse.

The doctor explained the options. I could do nothing, and things would get worse. I could have surgery to correct the problem. Or I could wear a brace, which would not correct the problem but might stop it from becoming any more serious. The doctor recommended the brace, and my parents and I agreed.

Getting measured for the brace was an ordeal. I had to hang from a bar while a man slopped a plaster mold on my body. After the cast hardened, he and his assistant placed me on a gurney so they could cut off the cast. The cast was so tight that I could hardly breathe. A few weeks later, the brace was ready.

Stainless steel and partially covered with leather, my Milwaukee Brace was a lovely contraption. It opened on hinges, allowing me to get in from the back. It fit snug around my hips and cinched up in the back. One metal bar extended up the front to my chin. Two smaller metal bars went up the back to my neck. A chin and neck rest were fastened to the bars and were fastened together with a type of round thumb nut. It held my head in place like one of those collars people wear for whiplash. When I grew and began to be not quite so uncomfortable in the thing, the doctor adjusted the headrest so I could be miserable again.

I wore the brace night and day for two and a half years. The only time I could take it off was when I bathed, which accounts for my spending a lot of free time in a bathtub even to this day. At the end of the two and a half years, the specialist examined X-rays and announced that the brace had not helped and I needed surgery after all. I wanted to see a new specialist.

My new doctor was on his way to Africa early in the summer, so we had to plan my surgery around his schedule. I would be operated on one week after my sophomore year ended, missing by one week a Scout trip to California. I would then wear a body cast and stay flat in bed for three months.

I had never had a broken bone or any stitches. I had hardly ever been ill. The only time I had spent in a doctor's office was for shots and checkups, and I had never spent time in a hospital. The thought of major surgery frightened me so badly that I couldn't eat. I lost weight and I couldn't sleep, but on a positive note, I got rid of the brace for almost a month before the surgery.

I checked into the hospital on a Tuesday and was operated on the following morning. When I became conscious again Wednesday evening, the first face I saw was that of my doctor. I thought I had awakened before the surgery and asked him when they were going to start. He said, "Start? You're all done." I remember thinking, "That wasn't so bad," but then the medication wore off.

For the next few days, I drifted in and out of consciousness, although I do remember the pain. Pillows were lined up on either side of me, and every half hour or so I had to be turned from my back to my side, from that side to my back, from my back to the other side. Three or four nurses usually eased me over with the help of a turn sheet and the pillows.

One evening when my mom was there, I asked to be turned. Mom told a nurse that I needed to be turned. She came in by herself and whipped the turn as if she were pulling a tablecloth out from under a table setting. I cried out in pain, and my couldn't-be-a-more-gentle-and-guileless, five-foot-two-inch mom was in the nurse's face! Mom ordered her out of the room, and I never saw that nurse again during my two-week stay. As Mormon might say, "Thus we see, don't mess with a mom protecting her children!"

A couple of weeks after the surgery, my parents brought me home. They carried me on a stretcher into the house and put me on a rented hospital bed. I could not walk. I was not even allowed to sit up or adjust the bed to more than a 20-degree incline. I was in a body cast and had to remain lying down for the remainder of the summer.

If I turned on my side, I could feed myself. Overeating caused incredible discomfort because a body cast cannot be loosened like a belt. Other than eating, I could do almost nothing for myself. It was humbling to have to rely on others for virtually everything. My dad fastened a bicycle horn to the headboard of the bed, and when I needed anything, I honked the horn and someone would come.

My little sister, Janean, got the brunt of doing everything for me. Turn the TV on. Change the channel. Get me a drink. Fetch me this. Bring me that. To her credit, she almost never complained. Well, there was that one time when someone brought me a dart gun with four darts and a target. I would fire the four darts at the target on the wall and then honk for Janean to pick up the darts and give them to me so I could shoot again. On her third or fourth trip in less than five minutes, she put her foot down.

Parenthetically, almost ten years later I was going through a box of stuff and found the bicycle horn. I held it in my hand, recalling that time of my life. Ending my reverie, I honked the horn and tossed it back in the box. A moment later Janean was at my doorway. She had heard the horn and automatically came in to see what I needed. Some might see this as a Pavlovian response. I saw it as dedicated service.

At the end of the summer, I went to the hospital to have the cast cut off. I was X-rayed, soaked in a hot tub, and then put in another body cast. I was allowed to sit, stand, and walk for the first time in nearly four months. It was painful and took some time to redevelop the muscles in my legs so I could walk normally. School started a week later, and I wore a body cast under my clothing for most of my junior year.

This was the most difficult trial I had ever faced. Clearly, many people have gone through far more painful and challenging circumstances. But in my young, self-centered mind, I could not imagine anyone suffering more than I was. I did not handle the adversity well. I complained, growled, grumbled, and moaned about my plight to anyone who would listen. My closest friends had to endure an almost nonstop barrage.

One day a good friend gave me wise council. "Shut up!" he said. "All you do is complain like you are the only one who ever had anything bad happen to him." He reminded me of several people our age who had had far more serious and painful things happen to them. He also reminded me that those people didn't complain or feel sorry for themselves. "They have good attitudes, and they are happy and fun to be around. And people like them!" I was an adversity wimp. It was a bitter pill to swallow.

What did I learn from this experience? The question I should have asked when all of this began was not "Why me?" but rather, "What can I learn from this?" or "How can I handle this well so I can mature spiritually?"

Let me quote again from Elder Scott's classic address on adversity from October 1995 general conference:

> When you face adversity, you can be led to ask many questions. Some serve a useful purpose; others do not. To ask, Why does this have to happen to me? Why do I have to suffer this, now? What have I done to cause this? will lead you into blind alleys. It really does no good to ask questions that reflect opposition to the will of God. Rather ask, What am I to do? What am I to learn from this experience? What am I to change? Whom am I to help? How can I remember my many blessings in times of trial? Willing sacrifice of deeply held personal desires in favor of the will of God is very hard to do. Yet, when you pray with real conviction, "Please let me know Thy will" and "May Thy will be done," you are in the strongest position to receive the maximum help from your loving Father.[9]

What did I learn from my curvature-of-the-spine experience? I gained a deeper appreciation for family, both immediate and extended family. They could not have been more patient, loving, and kind. And my friends were amazing. They hauled me outside on a stretcher for a type of back-yard campout, and we spent the night talking and laughing. I remember them designing a plan to load me into the back of a station wagon to take me to a drive-in movie. I couldn't do anything or go anywhere that summer, but my friends did not desert me.

I also learned that everyone faces challenges of various kinds. We must be patient in tribulation. We must remain as positive as we can, which requires faith and trust in God. President Hinckley quotes a newspaper article by Jenkins Lloyd Jones that he found meaningful:

> Anyone who imagines that bliss is normal is going to waste a lot of time running around shouting that he has been robbed. Most putts don't drop. Most beef is tough. Most children grow up to be just people. Most successful marriages require a high degree of mutual toleration. Most jobs are more often dull than otherwise. . . . Life is like an old-time rail journey—delays, sidetracks, smoke, dust, cinders and jolts, interspersed only occasionally by

beautiful vistas and thrilling bursts of speed. The trick is to thank the Lord for letting you have the ride.[10]

Even after acknowledging that most things do not go the way we planned and that life is often difficult and challenging, President Hinckley remains optimistic and encourages us to do the same. He also wrote:

> Looking at the dark side of things always leads to a spirit of pessimism which so often leads to defeat. . . . I have little doubt that many of us are troubled with fears concerning ourselves. We are in a period of stress across the world. There are occasionally hard days for each of us. Do not despair. Do not give up. Look for the sunlight through the clouds. Opportunities will eventually open to you. Do not let the prophets of gloom endanger your possibilities.[11]

As president of the Church, Gordon B. Hinckley wrote that in his ninety-plus years, he had learned a secret. "I have learned that when good men and good women face challenges with optimism, things will always work out! Truly, things always work out! Despite how difficult circumstances may look at the moment, those who have faith and move forward with a happy spirit will find that things always work out."[12]

Some years ago I read "The Uses of Adversity," an address given by Dr. Carlfred Broderick at a BYU women's conference—one of the best things I have ever read about dealing with adversity. In part, Dr. Broderick says:

> While I was a stake president, the event occurred that I want to use as the keynote to my remarks. I was sitting on the stand at a combined meeting of the stake Primary board and stake Young Women's board, where they were jointly inducting from the Primary into the Young Women organization the eleven-year-old girls who that year had made the big step. They had a lovely program. It was one of those fantastic, beautiful presentations, based on the Wizard of Oz, or a take-off on the Wizard of Oz, where Dorothy, an eleven-year-old girl, was coming down the yellow brick road together with the tin woodman, the

cowardly lion, and the scarecrow. They were singing altered lyrics about the gospel. And Oz, which was one wall of the cultural hall, looked very much like the Los Angeles temple. They really took off down that road. There were no weeds on that road; there were no munchkins; there were no misplaced tiles; there was no wicked witch of the west. That was one antiseptic yellow brick road, and it was very, very clear that once they got to Oz, they had it made. It was all sewed up.

Following that beautiful presentation with all the snappy tunes and skipping and so on, came a sister who I swear was sent over from Hollywood central casting. (I do not believe she was in my stake; I never saw her before in my life.) She looked as if she had come right off the cover of a fashion magazine—every hair in place, with a photogenic returned missionary husband who looked like he came out of central casting and two or three, or heaven knows how many, photogenic children, all of whom came out of central casting or Kleenex ads or whatever. She enthused over her temple marriage and how wonderful life was with her charming husband and her perfect children and that the young women too could look like her and have a husband like him and children like them if they would stick to the yellow brick road and live in Oz. It was a lovely, sort of tear-jerking, event.

After the event was nearly over, the stake Primary president, who was conducting, made a grave strategic error. She turned to me and, pro forma, said, "President Broderick, is there anything you would like to add to this lovely evening?"

I said, "Yes, there is," and I don't think she has ever forgiven me. What I said was this, "Girls, this has been a beautiful program. I commend the gospel with all of its auxiliaries and the temple to you, but I do not want you to believe for one minute that if you keep all the commandments and live as close to the Lord as you can and do everything right and fight off the entire priests quorum one by one and wait chastely for your missionary to return and pay your tithing and attend your meetings, accept calls from the bishop, and have a temple marriage, I do not want you to believe that bad things will not happen to you. And when that happens, I do not want you to say that God was not true. Or to say, 'They promised me in Primary, they promised me when I was a Mia Maid, they promised me from the pulpit that if I were very, very good, I would be blessed. But the boy I want doesn't know I exist, or the missionary I've waited for and kept chaste so we both could go to the temple turned out to be a flake,' or far worse things than any of the above. Sad things—children who are sick or developmentally handicapped, husbands who are not faithful, illnesses that can cripple, or violence, betrayals, hurts, deaths, losses—when those things happen, do not say God is not keeping His promises to me. The gospel of Jesus Christ is not insurance against pain. It is resource in the event of pain, and when that pain comes (and it will come because we came here on earth to have pain, among other things), when it comes, rejoice that you have resource to deal with your pain.[13]

Let us remember Brother Broderick's words: "The gospel of Jesus Christ is not insurance against pain. It is resource in the event of pain." When we use the resource of the gospel of Jesus Christ, we can do more than simply get through our trials. If we have faith and trust in God, our afflictions can be consecrated for our gain (see 2 Nephi 2:2), and we will mature spiritually.

### Notes

1. Richard G. Scott, "Trust in the Lord," *Ensign*, November 1995, 16.
2. Hinckley, *Teachings of Gordon B. Hinckley*, 6.
3. Kimball, *The Teachings of Spencer W. Kimball*, 511–12.
4. John Taylor, in *Journal of Discourses*, 14:360.
5. Neal A. Maxwell, "Swallowed Up in the Will of the Father," *Ensign*, November 1995, 24.
6. Richard G. Scott, "The Sustaining Power of Faith in Times of Uncertainty and Testing," *Ensign*, May 2003, 75.
7. Scott, "Trust in the Lord," 16–17.
8. Ibid., 19.

9. Ibid., 18.

10. Jenkins Lloyd Jones, "Big Rock Candy Mountains," *Deseret News,* June 12, 1973, A4.

11. "The Continuing Pursuit of Truth," *Ensign,* April 1986, 4.

12. Hinckley, *Way to Be,* 84.

13. Broderick, "The Uses of Adversity," 171–73.

# 12
# Hope

THE WORD *GOSPEL* MEANS "good news." The good news is that we can be saved. The gospel of Jesus Christ is Jesus saying to us, "I have good news. I can save you if you choose to be saved."

As we mature in our understanding of the Atonement of Christ and what is required of us to accept Jesus Christ as our Savior, we fulfill our part of the covenant and we enjoy hope. Unfortunately, many Latter-day Saints do not understand the good news and, consequently, do not feel the hope that comes with that understanding.

On at least one occasion, the apostles whom Jesus called during His mortal ministry struggled with the concern that salvation seemed unattainable. Three of the four gospels in the New Testament recount the story of a wealthy man who came to Jesus to ask what he needed to do to inherit eternal life. Jesus told him to keep the commandments. After the man explained that he had kept all of the commandments since he was young, he asked, "What lack I yet?"

Jesus responded, "If thou wilt be perfect, go and sell that thou hast, and give to the poor, . . . and come and follow me" (Matthew 19:16–21; Mark 10:17–27; Luke 18:27).

Hearing this, the man went away grieving because what he had was a lot. He was extremely rich, and he was unable to sacrifice his temporal possessions. After the wealthy man had departed, Jesus turned to his disciples and said, "Verily I say unto you, it is easier for a camel to go through the eye of a needle, than it is for a rich man to enter into the kingdom of God" (Matthew 19:24).

In *Jesus the Christ*, Elder James E. Talmage wrote that it had been asserted that the "eye of the needle" was a small gate or doorway set in or alongside the great gates of the city. He went on to say that "if this conception be correct," then a camel would have to be stripped of its burden and harness to be capable of entering this gate. Notice that Elder Talmage does not say that this is what the eye of the needle is, only that if it were true you could make some good analogies about people needing to rid themselves of pride and greed in order to enter God's kingdom.[1]

Elder Talmage likely got the gate concept from early Protestant writings in which certain theologians did not like the idea of a real camel actually having to pass through the eye of a needle because it was impossible. They came up with an explanation for what Jesus said that would make salvation difficult for a rich person but still possible. However, no historical evidence suggests that the eye of the needle refers to any type of gate or small entrance. So what did Jesus mean when He made the statement?

Another explanation comes from Bible interpreters who saw that the Greek word for *camel* and the Greek word for *rope* or *cable* differ only by a single letter. They suggested that perhaps the verse had been miscopied and mistranslated. Maybe what Jesus actually said was "It is easier for a rope to go through the eye of a needle." If this explanation is true, another analogy could be made that in order for a rope to pass through the needle's eye, it would have to be one strand at a time—little by little. This would be difficult but still possible. Other Bible scholars reject this explanation because it is common in ancient Jewish writings to find examples of a camel or even an elephant having to pass through the eye of a needle to evoke the feeling of an impossible situation.[2]

The point Jesus was making to his disciples was it is difficult, if not impossible, for people who cling to the world to enter into the kingdom of God. The disciples understood the reference and the level of difficulty Jesus expressed because they were exceedingly amazed and responded, "Who then can be saved?" They were saying, "If it is that difficult, how can *anyone* be saved? It sounds impossible!"

Jesus comforted them by saying, "With man this *is* impossible; but with God *all things are possible*" (Matthew 19:26; emphasis added). Or as the Joseph Smith Translation of Mark 10:26 reads: "With men that trust in riches, it is impossible; but not impossible with men who trust in God and leave all for my sake, for with such all these things are possible."

Some verses of scripture, if taken out of context or not read in conjunction with truths taught in other verses, can leave a person feeling hopeless. For example:

"I the Lord God cannot look upon sin with the least degree of allowance" (D&C 1:31).

"No unclean thing can inherit the kingdom of God" (Alma 40:26).

"For our words will condemn us, yea, all our works will condemn us; we shall not be found spotless; and our thoughts will also condemn us" (Alma 12:14).

"Have ye walked, keeping yourselves blameless before God? Could ye say, if ye were called to die at this time, within yourselves, that ye have been sufficiently humble? . . . Behold, are ye stripped of pride? I say unto you, if ye are not ye are not prepared to meet God" (Alma 5:27–28).

"If ye do not watch yourselves, and your thoughts, and your words, and your deeds, and observe the commandments of God, and continue in the faith . . . even unto the end of your lives, ye must perish" (Mosiah 4:30).

As I examine these verses and consider the necessary attributes required for celestial glory, I do not feel that I measure up to the qualifications of a celestial being. I am thankful for other verses found in the standard works that paint a more hopeful picture.

"For God so loved the world, that he gave his only begotten Son, that whosoever believeth in him should not perish, but have everlasting life" (John 3:16).

"He that believeth and is baptized shall be saved" (Mark 16:16).[3]

"In the world ye shall have tribulation: but be of good cheer; I have overcome the world" (John 16:33).

"For whatsoever is born of God overcometh the world: and this is the victory that overcometh the world, even our faith. Who is he that overcometh the world, but he that believeth that Jesus is the Son of God?" (1 John 5:3–5).

"Seek ye the kingdom of God; and all these things shall be added unto you. Fear not, little flock; for it is your Father's good pleasure to give you the kingdom" (Luke 12:31–32).

If we feel a sense of hopelessness as we read the scriptures, we are likely not reading with the Spirit. The Spirit brings hope. On the other hand, if we feel no sense of responsibility as we read the scriptures, no need or desire to repent, we are also reading them incorrectly. We must not feel content in our spirituality.

Nephi warns us, "Wo be unto him that is at ease in Zion!" (2 Nephi 28:24). It does not say, "Wo be unto him that is at *peace.*" He is merely saying that we all have work to do. Elder Neal A. Maxwell often called this feeling the need to change and improve "divine discontent."[4]

A lack of hope is not uncommon among youth and young single adults of the Church. I realized this a few years ago in a class of LDS young single adults, including a number of returned missionaries. We were discussing the great plan of happiness. One student outlined the plan on the board while the rest of the class helped flesh out the outline.

These young people were bright and well trained in the gospel. I thought everything was going well until we got to the degrees of glory. I've seen the typical plan of salvation illustrated many times, but I had never seen it done like this before. Here is how this young man drew the degrees of glory on the board that day:

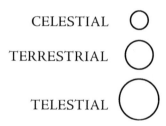

CELESTIAL

TERRESTRIAL

TELESTIAL

When I saw what he had drawn, I was confused and asked him, "What's with the snowman?" His response was, "Well, I drew it according to the number of people who will be in these kingdoms. There will be very few people who make it to the celestial kingdom. A lot of people will be going to the terrestrial kingdom. But the majority of people will be going to the telestial kingdom."

"Why would you think so few will be going to the celestial kingdom?" I asked.

In reply, he quoted a scripture: "Strait is the gate, and narrow is the way that leads to life, and few there be that find it" (3 Nephi 27:33). Another student added the scripture that says, "Be ye therefore perfect" (Matthew 5:48).

"Well, who do you think is going to make it to the celestial kingdom?" I asked.

A young lady answered, "The prophets and most of the apostles." I remember being surprised and saying, "*Most* of the apostles?"

"I imagine that all of today's apostles will make it," she said, "but there may be some from the early days of the Church who won't go to the celestial kingdom. You know, some who left the Church."

"All right, I understand what you are saying. Do you think that anyone besides the prophets and most of the apostles will end up in the celestial kingdom?"

Another girl responded, "Probably some really, really righteous stake presidents and bishops."

"Anyone else? What about somebody who is not in Church leadership?" I asked.

"Maybe a few incredibly righteous members of the Church," was the reply.

I asked, "What about you?" Silence filled the classroom. I remembered having attended a meeting years before where a member of the Quorum of the Twelve spoke to teachers from the Church Educational System. He noted that of all the things we teach the young people in our classes, we should make sure to teach them to have hope. I realized as I stood there in the class that few of these young people felt any hope of getting to the celestial kingdom.

In that institute class with the snowman on the board, I was blessed to answer some of the students' concerns about gaining exaltation. I had recently read *The Life Beyond*, a book that helped me see more clearly the goodness of God and the greatness of His merciful plan of happiness. "There is no ceiling on the number of saved beings," the authors wrote. "The design of God's plan is to save all who will be saved."[5] They cited the third article of faith, which states, "We believe that through the Atonement of Christ, *all mankind may be saved*" (emphasis added). The following is an excerpt from their book:

> In the long run, we must ever keep in mind that our God and Father is a successful parent, one who will save far more of his children than he will lose! If these words seem startling at first, let us reason for a moment. In comparison to the number of wicked souls *at any given time*, perhaps the numbers of faithful followers seem

small. But we must keep in mind how many of our spirit brothers and sisters—almost an infinite number—will be saved. What of the children who died before the age of accountability—billions of little ones from the days of Adam to the time of the Millennium? What of the billions of those who never had opportunity to hear the gospel message in mortality, but who afterwards received the glad tidings, this because of a disposition which hungered and thirsted after righteousness? And, might we ask, What of the innumerable hosts who qualified for exaltation from Enoch's city, from Melchizedek's Salem, or from the golden era of the Nephites? What of the countless billions of those children to be born during the great millennial era—during a time when disease and death have no sting or victory over mankind? This is that time of which we have spoken already, a season when "children shall grow up without sin unto salvation" (D&C 45:58). Given the renewed and paradisiacal state of the earth, it may well be that more persons will live on the earth during the thousand years of our Lord's reign— persons who are of at least a terrestrial nature—than the combined total of all who have lived during the previous six thousand years of the earth's temporal continuance. Indeed, who can count the number of saved beings in eternity? Our God, who is triumphant in all battles against the forces of evil, will surely be victorious in the numbers of his children who will be saved.[6]

In *Mediation and Atonement*, President John Taylor wrote that some in his day had estimated that more than half of the human family had died before reaching maturity.[7] A 1984 magazine article reported, "Of the seventy billion people who have been on the earth . . . 47 percent of males and 44 percent of females die before age eight. It follows that 46 percent of the earth's population (people ever born) are automatically exalted."[8]

We cannot know how accurate these estimates are, but we do know that billions of people have died before reaching the age of accountability. Doctrine and Covenants 137:10 states, "All children who die before they arrive at the years of accountability are saved in the celestial kingdom of heaven."

Now, I am *not* saying that the final outcome will look like this:

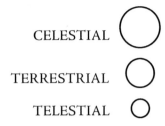

CELESTIAL

TERRESTRIAL

TELESTIAL

What I am saying is that our Father's plan will save many of His children. We know from Doctrine and Covenants, section 76, that the inhabitants of the telestial world, or lowest kingdom of glory, will be as innumerable as the stars in the heaven or the sand upon the seashore (v. 109). But would it be so surprising to find out that more of Heavenly Father's children are saved in the celestial kingdom than are not? Would it be so astonishing to discover that the celestial kingdom has more inhabitants than either of the other two kingdoms?

In a 1976 BYU devotional, Elder Bruce R. McConkie remarked:

> As members of the Church, if we chart a course leading to eternal life; if we begin the processes of spiritual rebirth, and are going in the right direction; if we chart a course of sanctifying our souls, and degree by degree are going in that direction; and if we chart a course of becoming perfect, and, step by step and phase by phase, are perfecting our souls by overcoming the world, then it is absolutely guaranteed—there is no question whatsoever about it—we shall gain eternal life. Even though we have spiritual rebirth ahead of us, perfection ahead of us, the full degree of sanctification ahead of us, if we chart a course and follow it to the best of our ability in this life, then when we go out of this life we'll continue in exactly that same course. . . . And in due course we'll get the fulness of our Father's kingdom. . . . I think we ought to have hope; I think we ought to have rejoicing.[9]

President Ezra Taft Benson warned us about the possibility of discouragement we might experience during the process of becoming like the Savior. He wrote:

We must be careful, as we seek to become more and more godlike, that we do not become discouraged and lose hope. Becoming Christlike is a lifetime pursuit and very often involves growth and change that is slow, almost imperceptible.... We must not lose hope. Hope is an anchor to the souls of men. Satan would have us cast away that anchor. In this way he can bring discouragement and surrender. But we must not lose hope. The Lord is pleased with every effort, even the tiny, daily ones in which we strive to be more like Him. Though we may see that we have far to go on the road to perfection, we must not give up hope.[10]

On another occasion, this time in a class with adults, we had a similar discussion. One woman said, "I feel okay about myself and most of my family. We are trying to do what is right, and I have faith in Christ and what His atonement does for us. But I am worried about one of my children, and I am very worried about my mother. I don't know if there is any hope for them."

This concern is common among Latter-day Saints: the worry that a few of our loved ones are not going to make it to the celestial kingdom. Several of the Brethren have addressed this issue in general conference in recent years. One of the best things that I have read was "Hope for Parents of Wayward Children" in the September 2002 *Ensign*. The article includes amazing statements by Joseph Smith, Brigham Young, and Lorenzo Snow that should give all of us great hope for those who have wandered from the faith. This statement from Elder Boyd K. Packer is included in the article:

The measure of our success as parents ... will not rest solely on how our children turn out. That judgment would be just only if we could raise our families in a perfectly moral environment, and that now is not possible. It is not uncommon for responsible parents to lose one of their children, for a time, to influences over which they have no control.... It is my conviction that those wicked influences one day will be overruled.[11]

We should understand two more aspects about hope. First, hope as used in the scriptures is not wishful thinking. It is not, "I sure *hope* I don't end up in hell." Hope as found in the scriptures is a feeling of assurance born of faith in Jesus Christ. It is peace felt in the soul. Scriptural hope is an actual expectation that we will make it to the celestial kingdom because we are on the right path, moving in the right direction, with a knowledge that the Savior is providing direction, correction, and grace. He will save us if we truly want to be saved.

Second, there is a very real connection among faith, hope, and charity. When we exercise *faith* in Jesus Christ by obeying laws and ordinances and when we truly obtain a brightness of *hope* in the Savior, then we *know* that, if we continue on the path, we will be saved. This knowledge does something wonderful. With this assurance in Christ, even though we still have to press forward and improve our lives, we don't have to worry about ourselves so much. And removing this worry and concern about our own salvation, we can focus on reaching out and helping others—or *charity*.

Let me illustrate what I mean with an analogy. I love sports. I know I shouldn't let games affect me so much, but I remember entire Christmas vacations being almost ruined because of a bad bowl game. But let me tell you what I have discovered: Saturday afternoon football on BYU television. On Saturday afternoons, this channel plays old football games. And the beauty of the games is that BYU never loses. Most of the games I have seen before. I watched many of them live in the stadium. But now as I watch, I don't get anxious or upset. If the Cougars are behind but look like they are driving for the winning touchdown and somebody fumbles—I'm okay. When I watched the game live, I wasn't okay with that fumble. It just about killed me.

So what is the difference? I know who is going to win. Things may look bleak. The other team may be way ahead at times, and it may look hopeless. But I know it isn't hopeless because I know who wins.

I also know—and so do you—who will win the war between good and evil. Members of the Godhead and all who follow them will win. So all we need to do is stay faithful and loyal to our Father in Heaven. Even if it sometimes appears as if Satan's forces are winning, they won't. Heavenly Father wins. It's a done deal. And we can win if we follow the Savior and return to our Father in Heaven.

Left on our own merits, what we earn and what we deserve, none of us can be saved. But with the atonement of Christ and His grace, each person who truly wants to be saved can be saved. "Wherefore, men are free according to the flesh; and all things are given them which are expedient unto man. And they are free to choose liberty and eternal life, through the great Mediator of all men, or to choose captivity and death, according to the captivity and power of the devil" (2 Nephi 2:27).

The hope spoken of in the scriptures comes from faith in Christ, confidence in the Father and His plan, and obedience to the laws and ordinances of the gospel. This assurance comes to us as we mature spiritually, having a greater understanding of God's plan for us and becoming more like our Father in Heaven and His Son. Then will our "confidence wax strong in the presence of God," and we will feel peace for ourselves and hope for our loved ones.

Notes

1. Talmage, *Jesus the Christ*, 485–86.

2. Farrar, *The Life of Christ*, 476.

3. "Salvation," or "being saved," in the scriptures almost always means exaltation. "Salvation in its true and full meaning is synonymous with exaltation or eternal life and consists in gaining an inheritance in the highest of the three heavens within the celestial kingdom. With few exceptions this is the salvation of which the scriptures speak" (McConkie, *Mormon Doctrine*, 670).

4. Neal A. Maxwell, "Consecrate Thy Performance," *Ensign*, May 2002, 36; "'According to the Desire of [Our] Hearts,'" *Ensign*, November 1996, 22; "'Settle This in Your Hearts,'" *Ensign*, November 1992, 66.

5. Millet and McConkie, *The Life Beyond*, 136.

6. Ibid., 137; emphasis in original.

7. Taylor, *The Mediation and Atonement*, 148.

8. Committee on Celestial Demographics, "In the Heavens, Are Parents Single?": Report No. 1, *Dialogue*, Spring 1984, 84–85.

9. Bruce R. McConkie, "Jesus Christ and Him Crucified," *1976 Devotional Speeches of the Year* (Provo, Utah: Brigham Young University Press, 1977), 400–401.

10. Ezra Taft Benson, "A Mighty Change of Heart," *Ensign*, October 1989, 5.

11. Boyd K. Packer, "Hope for Parents of Wayward Children," *Ensign*, September 2002, 11.

# 13

# Enduring to the End

WE ARE ADMONISHED MORE than a dozen times in the scriptures to endure to the end so that we can earn eternal life. "But he that shall endure unto the end, the same shall be saved" (Matthew 24:13). "If they endure unto the end they shall be lifted up at the last day, and shall be saved in the everlasting kingdom of the Lamb" (1 Nephi 13:37).

Elder Joseph B. Wirthlin referred to enduring to the end as one of the bedrock doctrines of the gospel of Jesus Christ. He said, "Some think of enduring to the end as simply suffering through challenges. It is so much more than that—it is the process of coming unto Christ and being perfected in Him."[1]

In the same verses that testify of the importance of enduring to the end, we learn that to endure means to have faith in Christ, repent, be baptized, be obedient to God's commandments, pray, follow the example of Jesus Christ in doing the Father's will, and "press forward, feasting upon the word of Christ" (2 Nephi 31:16, 20; see also 1 Nephi 22:31; 2 Nephi 9:24; Omni 1:26; D&C 14:7; D&C 18:22; D&C 20:25, 29).

A person cannot endure to the end of the path leading to exaltation until he gets on that path. We get on that path by having faith in Jesus Christ, repenting, being baptized by immersion for the remission of sins, and receiving the gift of the Holy Ghost through proper priesthood administration. Once on the path, we must continue "on the path leading to eternal life."[2]

The word *endure* suggests that life will not be easy. Scriptures do not mention coasting to the end or cruising or gliding to the end. Rather, the scripture counsel us to "be not weary in well doing" (Galatians 6:9; see also 2 Thessalonians 3:13; D&C 64:13).

The promise given in the Word of Wisdom that the Saints who walk "in obedience to the commandments . . . shall run and not be weary, and shall walk and not faint" (D&C 89:18, 20) refers to much more than our physical health. Notice that the scripture speaks of obedience to the *commandments,* not only the law known as the Word of Wisdom. Perhaps it means that by keeping the commandments of God we will not give out while we journey on the strait and narrow path but will be given the strength to endure.

It is troubling to see some returned missionaries become careless in their obedience of God's laws. While they served as missionaries, they worked hard to keep the commandments and live the mission rules. They prayed and studied the scriptures daily, and they bore strong testimonies of the truthfulness of the gospel. Their faith was firm, and their testimonies were real and powerful.

Upon return from their fields of missionary labor, these once humble and stalwart servants of the Lord stop doing the things that helped make them so strong when they were missionaries. They become lax in their prayers and cease studying the scriptures. Their resolve to keep the commandments wavers, and they begin to succumb to temptations.

They remember how firm their testimonies were. Some might even fool themselves into believing that they still have strong testimonies, but they are only living off the memory of a powerful testimony. When we face life's difficult challenges, the memory of a testimony is not enough to sustain us and help keep us on the path. The opposite of enduring to the end is *giving up*, and those who quit pressing forward and leave the path entirely will find that they have also *given up* "the greatest of all the gifts of God" (D&C 14:7)

We also face the danger in giving up when it comes to putting forth a sincere effort to consistently move forward on the path to eternal life. Some Latter-day Saints seem to be content with simply entering the path and setting up camp. We must remember that a path is meant to be walked. We must press forward on the path, with each step getting closer to our goal of returning to God and becoming like Him.

Enduring to the end is not a matter of perfect performance during our mortal sojourn, but it is having faith in Christ and pressing forward. When we fall to temptation, we take responsibility for our actions and get up to continue our journey on the path. The following poem illustrates the kind of effort needed to endure to the end.

## THE RACE
### Dee Groberg

"Quit! Give up! You're beaten!" They shout at me and plead.
"There's just too much against you now. This time you
    can't succeed."
And as I start to hang my head in front of failure's face,
My downward fall is broken by the memory of a race.
And hope refills my weakened will as I recall that scene;
For just the thought of that short race rejuvenates my being.
A children's race—young boys, young men—How I
    remember well.
Excitement, sure! But also fear; it wasn't hard to tell.
They all lined up so full of hope; each thought to win that race.
Or tie for first, or if not that, at least take second place.
And fathers watched from off the side, each cheering for his son.
And each boy hoped to show his dad that he could be the one.
The whistle blew and off they went, young hearts and hopes afire.
To win and be the hero there, was each young boy's desire.
And one boy in particular, whose dad was in the crowd,
Was running near the lead and thought: "My dad will be
    so proud!"
But as they sped down the field across the shallow dip,
The little boy who thought to win lost his step and slipped.
Trying hard to catch himself, his hands flew out to brace,
But 'mid the laughter of the crowd, he fell flat on his face.
So down he fell and with him hope. He couldn't win it now—

Embarrassed, sad, he only wished to disappear somehow.
But as he fell his dad stood up, and showed his anxious face,
Which to the boy so clearly said, "Get up and win the race."
He quickly rose, no damage done, behind a bit, that's all—
And ran with all his mind and might to make up for his fall.
So anxious to restore himself, to catch up and to win—
His mind went faster than his legs; he slipped and fell again!
He wished then he had quit before, with only one disgrace.
"I'm hopeless as a runner now; I shouldn't try to race."
But in the laughing crowd he searched and found his father's face;
That steady look that said again: "Get up and win the race!"
So he jumped up to try again, ten yards behind the last—
"If I'm to gain those yards," he thought, "I've got to move real fast."
Exerting everything he had, he regained eight or ten,
But trying so hard to catch the lead, he slipped and fell again!
Defeat! He lay there silently, a tear dropped from his eye.
"There's no sense running any more; three strikes: I'm out!
    Why try!"
The will to rise had disappeared; all hope had fled away;
So far behind, so error prone; a loser all the way.
"I've lost, so what's the use?" he thought. "I'll live with
    my disgrace."
But then he thought about his dad who soon he'd have to face.
"Get up," an echo sounded low. "Get up and take your place;
You were not meant for failure here. Get up and win the race.
"With borrowed will get up," it said. "You haven't lost at all.
For winning is no more than this: to rise each time you fall."
So up he rose to win once more, and with a new commit,
He resolved that win or lose at least he wouldn't quit.
So far behind the others now, the most he'd ever been,
Still he gave it all he had and ran as though to win.
Three times he'd fallen, stumbling; three times he rose again;
Too far behind to hope to win he still ran to the end.
They cheered the winning runner as he crossed the line first place.
Head high, and proud, and happy; no falling, no disgrace.
But when the fallen youngster crossed the line last place,
The crowd gave him the greater cheer, for finishing the race.
And even though he came in last, with head bowed low, unproud,

You would have thought he'd won the race to listen to the crowd.
And to his dad, he sadly said, "I didn't do too well."
"To me you won," his father said, "you rose each time you fell."
And now when things seem dark and hard and difficult to face,
The memory of that little boy helps me in my race.
For all of life is like that race, with ups and downs and all.
And all you have to do to win, is rise each time you fall.[3]

Speaking of the need to become perfect in order to gain exaltation, Elder McConkie shared these encouraging words:

> We don't have to get a complex or get a feeling that you have to be perfect to be saved. You don't. There's only been one perfect person, and that is the Lord Jesus. But in order to be saved in the Kingdom of God and in order to pass the test of mortality, what you have to do is get on the straight and narrow path—thus charting a course leading to eternal life—and then, being on that path, pass out of this life in full fellowship. . . . If you're on that path and pressing forward, and you die, you'll never get off the path. There is no such thing as falling off the straight and narrow path in the life to come, and the reason is that life is the time that is given to men to prepare for eternity.[4]

Elder Bruce R. McConkie taught that if we endure to the end of our mortal existence, staying on the path, we will remain on that path in the life to come. In *Mormon Doctrine*, he wrote, "To gain the promised inheritance in the celestial world it is necessary to travel the length of the path, a course of travel which consists in obedience to the laws and principles of the gospel. This process is called enduring to the end, *meaning the end of mortal life*."[5]

When we consider our goal of becoming like the Savior Jesus Christ, that task may seem daunting, even impossible. We are so weak, so imperfect, surrounded by sins and temptations "which do so easily beset" us (2 Nephi 4:18). No wonder at times we might feel that our chances for exaltation are bleak. But if we are asked, "Can you stay on the path? Can you press forward, repent, and become a better person? Can you leave this life a faithful member of The Church of Jesus Christ of Latter-day Saints?" We can do that. According to Elder McConkie, that would be sufficient:

> What you do have to do is stay in the mainstream of the Church and live as upright and decent people live in the Church—keeping the commandments, paying your tithing, serving in the organizations of the Church, loving the Lord, staying on the straight and narrow path. If you're on that path and death comes—because this is the time and the day appointed, this is the probationary estate—you'll never fall off from it, and for all practical purposes, your calling and election is made sure.[6]

Think of it. If you are on the path, pressing forward and living a worthy life, at death you will continue on the path and ultimately receive your exaltation. It is not a matter of achieving perfection in this life but of becoming worthy and then maintaining that worthiness to the conclusion of our mortality.

So what does it mean to be worthy?

I had an enlightening experience when I was interviewing for a temple recommend with my stake president, whom I knew well. He asked the temple recommend questions, and I responded appropriately. Near the end of the interview, he asked if I considered myself worthy to enter the temple. I am nowhere near perfect and, feeling these imperfections, I told him I did not consider myself worthy. He hesitated, looked me straight in the eyes, and asked, "Which of the questions I asked did you lie in your answer?"

"I did not lie to you on any of the questions."

He responded, "Then why don't you consider yourself worthy? I did not ask if you were perfect; I asked if you were worthy."

"I guess I don't really know what worthiness means," I replied.

My stake president taught me that worthiness does not mean there are no sins or imperfections in our lives but that we have no serious transgressions that would keep us out of the temple or put our Church membership in question. He explained that being worthy means we are living at least the minimum requirements so that we can enter the house of the Lord to continue our personal progression toward greater righteousness.

Enduring to the end is our final step in mortality to becoming spiritually mature. We prepare ourselves to get on the path leading back to our Father's presence through faith, repentance, and covenanting to be obedient. We enter the path through baptism and receiving the gift of the Holy Ghost. We walk the path by keeping the covenants we made at baptism, then making more covenants with God in the temple and keeping those covenants as well.

We progress farther on the path by receiving and following the promptings of the Holy Ghost and by feasting on the words of Christ. If we can do these things to the end of our mortal lives, we have endured to the end and will receive the blessings of eternity. "Wherefore, if ye shall press forward, feasting upon the word of Christ, and endure to the end, behold, thus saith the Father: Ye shall have eternal life" (2 Nephi 31:20).

Notes

1. Joseph B. Wirthlin, "Press On," *Ensign*, November 2004, 101.
2. Ibid.
3. Groberg, *The Race: Life's Greatest Lesson.*
4. Bruce R. McConkie, "The Probationary Test of Mortality," transcript of an unpublished address given at the Salt Lake Institute adjacent to the University of Utah, January 10, 1982, 9.
5. McConkie, *Mormon Doctrine*, 228; emphasis added.
6. McConkie, "The Probationary Test of Mortality," address given at the Salt Lake Institute of Religion, University of Utah, January 10, 1982, 9.

# Conclusion

THE SUMMER AFTER I turned twelve, I went with the Boy Scouts to camp for a week. The day after we arrived, camp leaders met with the scouts from each camp to explain a problem and ask for help. The leaders told us that the camp was being overrun with porcupines that were damaging many of the trees in the area. They said that if we came across a porcupine during our stay, we were to dispatch it immediately. They even suggested that we organize troop porcupine hunts.

"Where are the guns?" we all wanted to know excitedly. The thought of several hundred armed twelve- to sixteen-year-olds traipsing through the woods seemed to upset them.

"Oh, no," the head camp leader explained quickly, "no one gets a gun. You kill the porcupines with a club." He went on to explain that the porcupine has a sharp nose bone, and all we needed to do was rap the critter on the nose. The bone would pierce the brain, and the animal would die instantly. Before you begin to worry, let me report that no porcupines are injured in this story. In fact, no one even *saw* a porcupine the entire time we were there. I rather believe that it was all a clever ploy by the camp leadership to keep us busy all week.

An interesting thing did develop as the week progressed, however. Porcupines were forgotten, but a contest as to who had the best club emerged. Scouts sanded and carved words, pictures, and designs on their clubs. I was caught up in club fever myself and spent several hours scouring the woods for the perfect fallen branch with which to make my club. Each time I thought I'd found one that was just right, I'd find that it wasn't as straight as I wanted or as thick as I needed. Some limbs were too big. Others were covered with dirt or mud.

It only took me a few hours to realize that I was not going to find a perfectly made Louisville Slugger lying in the forest. What I needed to do was find a piece of wood that I could work with and make the way I wanted it.

I share this incident for several reasons. First, many of life's experiences can become teaching moments if we will open our spiritual eyes to the fact that mortality is a place of learning. It was not until years after the porcupine club episode that I recognized what had happened as a meaningful parable for me.

An individual was called to a position of leadership within the stake where I lived, and the murmuring commenced. "Why would they choose him? I don't think that he is right for the job. There are so many others who are more qualified than he is."

Although I did not say anything to anyone, the thought occurred to me that he was not exactly perfect for that position. At that moment, the memory of what had happened at scout camp flashed into my mind. It seemed very strange at first that while thinking about a person's new Church calling, I would recall a scout camp experience from my youth, but then the connection hit me. When I was walking through the forest looking for the perfect club, many looked promising until I picked them up and examined them carefully. Each time I saw flaws, things that were imperfect.

Who is perfect for any calling? If another person had been selected out of the congregation and called to that position instead, would people have noticed the other person's flaws and would there still have been murmuring? Just as there are no Louisville Sluggers lying in the woods, so there are no perfect people with whom Heavenly Father can staff His Church. There are only people with the potential of being right for the job as God works with them and smooths their rough edges.

Joseph Smith likened himself to a large stone rolling down from high on a mountain. The Prophet said that he was being polished when "some corner gets rubbed off by coming into contact with something else, striking with accelerated force . . . all hell knocking off a corner here and a corner there. Thus I will become a smooth and polished shaft in the quiver of the Almighty."[1]

I think of the porcupine club when I have received callings in the Church that I feared might be too challenging. As strong feelings of inadequacy have washed over me, I have been able to say, "I may not be the best person for the assignment, but I have been called by God and, with effort on my part and His help, I can become the person He wants me to be."

Another reason for sharing this story is to point out the importance of not judging the spiritual maturity of others. The Savior instructed His disciples that they should not judge unrighteously, "for with what judgment ye shall judge, ye shall be judged" (JST, Matthew 7:2–3,). Jesus' message of the mote and the beam is a perfect reminder that we all need to focus more on our own spiritual shortcomings than on the weaknesses of others.

Elder Neal A. Maxwell taught:

> One of the realities of the kingdom is that we work with each other in the midst of our imperfections. We see those imperfections as well as the traits and talents that God has blessed us with. And during this process of life together in the community of Saints, we watch each other grow.[2]

We need to pay more attention to and show greater appreciation for the strengths and growth of others, while being extremely tolerant for their lack of strength in other areas. We expect others to be lenient with us, and so we must be equally compassionate with them.

Bishops are called to be judges in Israel, but they know the difference between having a stewardship to be a judge and being judgmental. Parents also have a stewardship and should be concerned with the spiritual maturing process of their children. Sometimes parents forget that their children are not far along in their mortal progression simply because of fewer experiences and a shorter time on the earth.

My mom was irritated with some of my immature antics on one occasion and then realized that perhaps she was expecting too much from me at that time. She said to me, "You're acting like you are sixteen."

"I *am* sixteen," I responded, somewhat bewildered.

"I know," she said, "I know." And then she gave me a hug, leaving me even more confused.

Speaking to young single adults, Elder Maxwell said:

> I hope you will forgive me if I say something your
> parents might like to say, because I can do it better than
> they. I can remember three or four times when I was a
> little feisty and independent before marriage—not as to
> behavioral or doctrinal things, just more assertive—and
> while my parents saw that, they respected my agency. I
> knew how they felt, but they backed off a little bit. There
> was almost a sacred zone there where they could say, "You
> know how we feel."
>
> I found myself loving and respecting them all the
> more. If some of you may be in that situation now or
> subsequently, and see in your wonderful parents a
> willingness to back off a little bit because they honor
> your agency, honor them. Back off a little bit, and out
> of that will come the kind of negotiation you'll come
> to expect a little more when you are on the other side
> of that equation.[3]

The calling of parents is to teach their children "to understand the
doctrine of repentance, faith in Christ the Son of the living God, and of
baptism and the gift of the Holy Ghost by the laying on of hands" (D&C
68:25). Parents are responsible for helping their children get on the path
that leads them back to the presence of God. They also are commissioned
by the Lord to encourage their children to stay on that path. "And they
shall also teach their children to pray, and to walk uprightly before the
Lord" (D&C 68:28). Parents need to be helpful and supportive without
being overcritical or judgmental.

We came to this earth to become like our Father in Heaven. In order
to do that, we needed a physical body and we needed to experience life and
pass the tests and challenges that each individual faces during mortality.
Experience is important, but experience alone is not sufficient. We must
learn from our experience. We must recognize eternal truths, or many of
our experiences will have been for naught.

The only people who don't have to pass the test to gain their exaltation
are those who don't become accountable in this life either because they
die before they become accountable or they do not reach the mental age
of accountability. Through the atonement of Christ, these people remain

under "celestial warranty" and will receive their exaltation in the celestial kingdom. The rest of us need to mature spiritually.

It is not enough simply to be a member of The Church of Jesus Christ of Latter-day Saints. We must be valiant in our efforts to come unto Christ. Some years ago I had an interesting experience when I was serving in a bishopric. One Sunday the bishop invited me into the office after sacrament meeting to talk about some urgent items of business. During our discussion, there came a knock at the door. A Sunday School teacher of older teenagers had struggled to teach her class while two young men went out of their way to disturb everyone. After several efforts to quiet them, the teacher had asked them to leave, and they wouldn't even do that. So she brought them to the bishop's office. The bishop invited the young men in, and I started to leave, but the bishop asked me to stay.

This gentle, mild-mannered bishop attempted to explain to these young men the importance of listening to gospel teachings and being respectful of the teacher and other students. The two young men were belligerent in their demeanor and in their comments, but the bishop remained caring and patient. I was impressed by the bishop's concern for the young men and his control while they treated him with such disrespect.

I witnessed the spirit of discernment move upon that bishop as he used Lehi's dream and likened it to their situation. He concluded the analogy with a plea for them to come unto the tree and partake of the fruit. He bore witness of the sweetness of the fruit and the joy that it brings.

One of the boys said, "Look, don't give us that junk about the iron rod and the tree and how great the fruit is. We come to Church every week, just like you. We sit through sacrament meeting and our classes, just like you. We've been baptized and received the gift of the Holy Ghost. We've both got the Aaronic Priesthood. We go home teaching and take care of the sacrament. We have come to the tree and we've tasted the fruit, and I've got news for you, it isn't that good!"

The bishop sat silent for a moment, with sadness in his eyes. With gentleness still in his voice, he replied, "You really don't get it at all. Yes, you have been baptized and confirmed. You attend your meetings and do some Church assignments. Maybe you really believe that you have come unto the tree, but I can tell you this: you have never tasted the fruit. If anything, you have just been chewing on the bark."

I know that "it is by grace that we are saved, after all we can do" (2 Nephi 25:23). The Savior has done His part, and the Atonement is in place. Our main concern should be what we can do now. Are we progressing and growing and learning? Are we better people now than we used to be? Do we continue to put forth sincere efforts to improve?

Paul wrote of putting away childish things. Are there still childish things in our lives that need to be put away? Are we *growing up* in the gospel? Are we developing spiritual maturity?

Notes

1. Smith, *Teachings of the Prophet Joseph Smith*, 304.
2. Neal A. Maxwell, "Sharing Insights from My Life," *Brigham Young University 1998–99 Speeches* (Provo, Utah: University Publications, 1999), 114.
3. Ibid., 116.

# Bibliography

Asay, Carlos E. *In the Lord's Service: A Guide to Spiritual Development.* Salt Lake City, Deseret Book, 1990.

Ashton, Marvin J. *The Measure of Our Hearts.* Salt Lake City: Deseret Book, 1991.

Benson, Ezra Taft. *The Teachings of Ezra Taft Benson.* Salt Lake City: Bookcraft, 1988.

Bible Dictionary. Located in the LDS Edition of the Holy Bible. Salt Lake City: The Church of Jesus Christ of Latter-day Saints, 1979.

Broderick, Carlfred. "The Uses of Adversity." In *As Women of Faith: Talks Selected from the BYU Women's Conferences.* Salt Lake City: Deseret Book, 1989.

Callister, Tad R. *The Infinite Atonement.* Salt Lake City: Deseret Book, 2000.

*Collected Discourses, 1886–1898.* 5 volumes. Compiled and edited by Brian H. Stuy. Burbank, California, and Woodland Hills, Utah: B. H. S. Publishing, 1987–1992.

Conference Reports of The Church of Jesus Christ of Latter-day Saints. Salt Lake City: The Church of Jesus Christ of Latter-day Saints, 1898 to present.

Eyring, Henry B., ed. *On Becoming a Disciple-Scholar.* Salt Lake City: Bookcraft, 1995.

Farrar, Frederic W. *The Life of Christ.* Portland, Oregon: Fountain Publications, 1964.

Groberg, Dee. *The Race: Life's Greatest Lesson.* New York: Time Warner Book Group, 2004.

Hinckley, Gordon B. *Teachings of Gordon B. Hinckley.* Salt Lake City: Deseret Book, 1997.

_____. *Way to Be.* New York: Simon and Schuster, 2002.

Holland, Jeffrey R., and Patricia T. Holland. *On Earth As It Is in Heaven.* Salt Lake City: Deseret Book, 1989.

Hunter, Howard W. *The Teachings of Howard W. Hunter.* Edited by Clyde J. Williams. Salt Lake City: Bookcraft, 1997.

*Journal of Discourses.* 26 volumes. London: Latter-day Saints' Book Depot, 1854–86.

Kimball, Spencer W. *The Teachings of Spencer W. Kimball.* Edited by Edward L. Kimball. Salt Lake City: Bookcraft, 1982.

Lee, Harold B. *The Teachings of Harold B. Lee.* Edited by Clyde J. Williams. Salt Lake City: Bookcraft, 1996.

Maxwell, Neal A. "The Disciple-Scholar." In *On Becoming a Disciple-Scholar.* Edited by Henry B. Eyring. Salt Lake City: Bookcraft, 1995.

_____. *A More Excellent Way.* Salt Lake City: Deseret Book, 1973.

_____. *Men and Women of Christ.* Salt Lake City: Bookcraft, 1991.

_____. *Notwithstanding My Weakness.* Salt Lake City: Deseret Book, 1981.

_____. *That Ye May Believe.* Salt Lake City: Bookcraft, 1992.

McConkie, Bruce R. *Doctrinal New Testament Commentary.* 3 volumes. Salt Lake City: Bookcraft, 1965-1973.

_____. *Doctrines of the Restoration: Sermons and Writings of Bruce R. McConkie.* Edited by Mark L. McConkie. Salt Lake City: Bookcraft, 1989.

_____. *Mormon Doctrine.* 2d ed. Salt Lake City: Bookcraft, 1966.

_____. *The Promised Messiah: The First Coming of Christ.* Salt Lake City: Deseret Book, 1978.

Millet, Robert L. and Joseph Fielding McConkie. *The Life Beyond.* Salt Lake City: Bookcraft, 1986.

Oaks, Dallin H. "On Learning and Becoming." In *On Becoming a Disciple-Scholar.* Henry B. Eyring, ed. Salt Lake City: Bookcraft, 1995.

_____. *The Lord's Way.* Salt Lake City: Deseret Book, 1991.

Packer, Boyd K. *Let Not Your Heart Be Troubled.* Salt Lake City: Salt Lake City: Bookcraft, 1991.

_____. *That All May Be Edified.* Salt Lake City: Bookcraft, 1982.

Pratt, Parley P. *Key to the Science of Theology/A Voice of Warning.* Salt Lake City: Deseret Book, 1978.

Romney, Marion G. *Look to God and Live: Discourses of Marion G. Romney.* Compiled by George J. Romney. Salt Lake City: Deseret Book, 1975.

Smith, Joseph. *Teachings of the Prophet Joseph Smith.* Selected by Joseph Fielding Smith. Salt Lake City: Deseret Book, 1976.

_____. *History of the Church of Jesus Christ of Latter-day Saints.* Edited by B. H. Roberts. 2d ed. rev. 7 volumes. Salt Lake City: The Church of Jesus Christ of Latter-day Saints, 1932–51.

Smith, Joseph F. *Gospel Doctrine.* Salt Lake City: Deseret Book, 1973.

Talmage, James E. *Jesus the Christ: A Study of the Messiah and His Mission According to Holy Scriptures both Ancient and Modern.* Salt Lake City: Deseret Book, 1970.

Taylor, John. *The Mediation and Atonement*. Reprint of 1882 edition. Salt Lake City: Deseret News Company, 1973.

Woodruff, Wilford. *The Discourses of Wilford Woodruff*. Edited by G. Homer Durham. Salt Lake City: Bookcraft, 1969.

Young, Brigham. *Discourses of Brigham Young*. Selected and arranged by John A. Widtsoe. Salt Lake City: Deseret Book, 1969.

_____. *Manuscript History of Brigham Young 1846–1847*. Edited by Elden J. Watson. Salt Lake City: Elden J. Watson, 1971.

# Index

# About the Author

Richard G. Moore grew up in Salem, Utah. After serving as a missionary in Japan, he graduated from Brigham Young University with a bachelor's degree in American history. Richard also received a master's degree in history from BYU and a doctorate in educational administration from the University of the Pacific.

He has been a speaker for Know Your Religion and Education Week. He was a seminary teacher in Arizona and Utah, a Church Educational System coordinator and institute director in northern California, and is currently an institute instructor at the Orem Institute of Religion.

Richard has taught for more than thirty years in the Church Educational System. He and his wife, Lani, have three children: Adam, Travis, and Asia.